Dear God, I Have a Question

honest answers to kids' questions about faith

Kathryn Slattery

Tommy Nelson®
An Imprint of Thomas Nelson

HC CB
HARPERCOLLINS CHILDREN'S BOOKS

For dear Sebastian, and children of all ages everywhere.

This edition published in India in 2024 by HarperCollins Children's Books
An imprint of HarperCollins *Publishers*
Building No 10, Tower A, 4th Floor, DLF Cyber City, Phase II,
Gurugram - 122002
www.harpercollins.co.in

P-ISBN: 978-93-6213-025-9

Published by arrangement with HarperCollins Focus, LLC

Dear God, I Have a Question

Tommy Nelson, PO Box 141000, Nashville, TN 37214

Portions of this book were previously published in *If I Could Ask God Anything*, © 2006, 2010, and *365 Bible Answers for Curious Kids*, © 2017.

Published in Nashville, Tennessee, by Tommy Nelson. Tommy Nelson is an imprint of Thomas Nelson. Thomas Nelson is a registered trademark of HarperCollins Christian Publishing, Inc.

Published in association with the literary agency of Mark Sweeney & Associates, Carol Stream, Illinois 60188.

Tommy Nelson titles may be purchased in bulk for educational, business, fund-raising, or sales promotional use. For information, please e-mail SpecialMarkets@ThomasNelson.com.

Illustrated by Carolina Farías

Library of Congress Cataloging-in-Publication Data

Names: Slattery, Kathryn, author.
Title: Dear God, I have a question: honest answers to kids' questions about faith / Kathryn Slattery.
Description: Nashville, TN : Tommy Nelson, Thomas Nelson, 2020. | "Portions of this book were previously published in If I Could Ask God Anything, ©2006, 2010, and 365 Bible Answers for Curious Kids, © 2017." | Audience: Ages 6-10 | Summary: "Dear God, I Have a Question, by beloved Bible teacher Kathryn Slattery, helps you and your kids find biblical answers to a child's toughest questions about God, Christianity, the Bible, heaven, and so much more"-- Provided by publisher.
Identifiers: LCCN 2020010137 (print) | LCCN 2020010138 (ebook) | ISBN 9781400223268 (softcover) | ISBN 9781400223244 (epub)
Subjects: LCSH: Christianity--Miscellanea--Juvenile literature.
Classification: LCC BR125.5 .S525 2020 (print) | LCC BR125.5 (ebook) | DDC 230--dc23
LC record available at https://lccn.loc.gov/2020010137
LC ebook record available at https://lccn.loc.gov/2020010138

Printed and bound at Thomson Press (India) Ltd

Contents

Note to Grown-Ups

• • • • • • •

Children, like grown-ups, need faith. We are now living in what historians and many theologians call the "post-Christian" age. Secular humanism, moral relativism, materialism, and political correctness have created a moral atmosphere of murky gray where there are few absolutes to help parents and children discern right from wrong. The advent of the internet and social media has only added to the confusion with their persistent, powerful voices, relentlessly competing for our children's attention, hearts, and minds. Even the way we do something as fundamental as note the passage of time has been secularly redefined. In academic circles, BC, which traditionally stands for "before Christ," has been replaced by the more politically correct BCE, or "before the common era." Likewise, AD, which stands for the Latin *anno Domini*, or "in the year of our Lord," has been replaced by CE, or "of the common era."

Today more than ever, children need to be informed and reassured that God is real, that He personally loves them, and that He has a unique purpose for each of their lives. What the late, great Christian apologist C. S. Lewis called "mere Christianity" can make a powerful, positive difference in a child's life. Young people can be motivated and empowered by faith to make a positive difference in a fallen and hurting world. Children can and should be able to articulate what they believe and why they believe it.

We can rejoice that children enter this world with a tremendous capacity for faith. For children, believing in God is instinctive. It is as natural as breathing. As Jesus said, "Let the little children come to me, and do not hinder them, for the kingdom of God belongs to such as these" (Mark 10:14; Luke 18:16 NIV).

It is not only our privilege but also our responsibility to nurture our children's God-given faith. Typically, our children's Christian education includes involvement in Sunday school, familiarity with the Bible, and routine prayers at meals and bedtimes. But that's not really enough. It takes a personal, intimate relationship with a loving God to breathe life and meaning into these religious traditions. As a Sunday school teacher, I was stunned to discover how little my students knew about the basics of the Christian faith, let alone about the Bible and the church.

Written for children of all denominations, *Dear God, I Have a Question* offers clear, fresh, honest answers in language that kids can understand to a wide variety of questions that ultimately cover the basic tenets of biblically based orthodox Christianity, such as:

How can I know God is real?
Why was Jesus killed?
How can God be three persons at the same time?
How can I know for sure that Jesus really was resurrected?
What is Communion?

It also includes answers to fun and challenging questions such as:

What did Jesus look like?
Is there really a lost ark of the covenant?
Are there really angels?
Did Jesus really walk on water?
Is it okay to pray for help on a test?

Dear God, I Have a Question will deepen young readers' understanding of how faith works in their own lives and help them see how they fit into the larger body of Christ at work in the world today and throughout history. Most important, this book is written with the aim of helping young readers establish a deep and lasting personal relationship with a living, loving God through faith in Jesus Christ.

Dear God, I Have a Question is, quite frankly, a book I wish my two children had had when they were young. It is also a book I wish I'd had during my many years teaching Sunday school. Now that I am a grandmother, I am very excited at the thought of how grandparents too will find *Dear God, I Have a Question* a tremendous resource.

I encourage you to explore the questions in this book with your child and grow in faith together. And don't be surprised when your child teaches you!

There are, of course, an infinite number of questions about God—more than could ever be answered in one book. When your child comes to you with difficult questions, you may find that your own faith is challenged. When there seems to be no satisfactory answer for a question, don't be afraid to say, "I don't know," or "Let's look in the Bible," or "Let's ask our pastor about that."

In the end, you and your child will gain a clearer understanding of exactly what you believe and why. Remember, God loves a seeking heart (Matthew 7:7–12).

And God loves you.

Kathryn Slattery

Bedford, New Hampshire

GOD

Who Is God?

• • • • • • •

God is the Creator of everything, visible and invisible. God created heaven and the angels. He created time and space. From God's fingertips tumbled galaxies, the stars, and our beautiful planet. God loved His creation so much that He didn't stop there. He went on to create the oceans, animals, birds in the sky, and fish in the sea. At the end of each day of creation, God saw that it was good (Genesis 1, verses 10, 12, 18, 21, and 25).

As His final act of creation, God created the first human man and woman, Adam and Eve. God was so pleased with them that He could barely contain His joy. Looking at Adam and Eve and all that He had made, God saw that it was not only good but "very good" (Genesis 1:31)! It is easy to imagine God's eyes sparkling with love and pride.

Guess who else God created?

God created you!

God created all the people on earth, people who are living and people who have died. God loves each of them and knows everything about them, including people who haven't been born yet (Psalm 139:13–16).

God is your loving Creator.

Where Did God Come From?

• • • • • • •

The Bible says that God is both the beginning and the end (Revelation 21:6). This is because God is eternal. The word *eternal* means endless. How can God be eternal?

God is uncreated. God is not limited by time and space. God existed before the dawn of time. God created time!

God is unchanging. He is the same today as He was yesterday. He will be the same tomorrow. This is a hard idea for our human minds to understand. But it is true. You can always count on God!

God is eternal.
***Eternal* means**
endless.

How Can I Know God Is Real?

We can't see some things with our eyes, yet we know they are real. We can't see gravity, but it is real. How do we know? Because if you let go of this book, it will drop to the floor with a big thud! We can't see electricity, but it powers our lights.

My favorite example is the wind. We can't see it, but we can feel it when it cools our skin on a hot summer day. We can see treetops swaying and clouds racing across the sky. God is like the wind. Even though we can't see God, we can feel His hugs and hear His loving voice in our hearts.

More than anything, God wants you to know that He is real and that He loves you. You are special! No one is quite like you. And God has a very special purpose for your life.

Who Is the Trinity?

• • • • • • •

The Bible teaches that God is made up of three Persons (Matthew 28:19):

1. God
2. God's Son, Jesus
3. God's Holy Spirit

The word *trinity* means "three in one."

The Trinity is a way to describe God. Even though Jesus didn't use the word *trinity*, He was the first person to speak clearly about it (Matthew 28:19). We have hints of the Trinity even as far back as the very first book in the Bible. Genesis says that when God made the world, He said, "Let *us* make mankind in *our* image, in *our* likeness" (1:26 NIV). Isn't that amazing? Although Jesus would not arrive on earth for thousands of years, Jesus and the Holy Spirit *were with and part of God* since before the dawn of time.

How Can God Be Three Persons at the Same Time?

No doubt about it, the idea of God being three Persons at the same time is hard to understand. That's because God's thoughts and ways are so different and so much higher than ours. We are humans. God is God! He knows everything!

But we can still try to understand how God can be three in one. Take an egg, for example. It has three parts—the shell, the white, and the yolk—but they're all part of the same egg. What about your family? You might be a daughter, a niece, and a sister all at the same time. Or think about water. When water is room temperature, it's a flowing liquid. When heated in a teakettle, it becomes steam. When frozen, it becomes ice. But it is always water.

Although these examples are not perfect, I hope they help you understand how God can be three persons at the same time.

How Is My Heavenly Father Different from My Parents?

• • • • • • • • •

Every child begins life with a biological or earthly mother and father. Some children are raised by their biological earthly parents. Some children are raised by adoptive earthly parents. Unlike God, human moms and dads are not perfect. They make mistakes. They can get tired and grumpy. They can have problems and get divorced. Earthly parents can get hurt or sick or even die.

> **The Father has loved us so much! He loved us so much that we are called children of God.**
>
> **—1 JOHN 3:1**

The good news is that every child also has a spiritual Parent—our Father God in heaven.

God loves us perfectly and never gets tired, grumpy, or sick. Best of all, God never dies—or changes. He is the same today as He was yesterday and will be tomorrow (Hebrews 13:8)! You can always count on God.

Know this: *God always has time for you.* Whenever you call God's name, out loud or silently, it is like you are the only person in the world, and God turns His total attention to you. Why? Because God loves you perfectly. We are *never* inconvenient to our Father God. This is because God's love for us is perfect.

Who is God? He is your Creator and your perfect Parent. What is the best word to describe God? God is *love* (1 John 4:8).

What Is the Kingdom of God?

• • • • • • •

The "kingdom of God" is another way to say *heaven*. Although we can't see heaven, the Bible tells us that it is real and wonderful! Heaven is home for God; His Son, Jesus; the Holy Spirit; God's angels; and all human believers in Jesus. Many theologians believe that heaven "breaks through" to earth every day, in ways large and small. A *theologian* is a person who studies God. The biggest breakthrough happened when God sent Jesus into human history to save and change the world forever! Three days after His death on the cross, Jesus miraculously rose from the dead with a brand-new heavenly body designed to live forever. Forty days later, Jesus *ascended* or "went up" to heaven, where He lives and rules as our heavenly King.

"God's kingdom is within you."
—LUKE 17:21

Thanks to Jesus, one day we too, will receive new bodies and join God and Jesus in heaven. For now, we have the gift of God's Holy Spirit living in our hearts, helping us share God's love with others here on earth. That's what Jesus meant when He said, "God's kingdom is within you" (Luke 17:21). This is very good news!

GOD AND ME

What Does God See When He Looks at Me?

• • • • • • •

When God looks at you, He sees you busy living your everyday life. He sees you sitting at your desk in school, riding your bike, watching TV, surfing the internet, and eating dinner. He sees you sleeping too. This is not surprising, because God is your loving Creator and heavenly Father.

But God also sees the *inside* of you (1 Chronicles 28:9; 1 Samuel 16:7). In fact, God is more interested in who you are on the inside than in what you are on the outside. This is because what's inside you is eternal—which means it lasts forever and ever. Who you are on the inside is called your *soul.* Your soul is made up of your unique personality—all your thoughts, feelings, dreams, hopes, interests, and knowledge. It's the love in your heart. Do you try to be kind? Are you honest? Do you like to laugh? This is what's important to God.

When God looks at you, He loves you completely—inside and out.

God loves you so much that He wants you to live forever with Him in heaven (John 3:16)!

What Does It Mean to Be Created in the Image of God?

• • • • • • •

The Bible says that human beings are created "in the image of God" (Genesis 1:27). Because you are God's child, you are like your heavenly Father in many ways:

- Because God is loving, you can be loving.
- Because God has a sense of humor, you can laugh.
- Because God is joyful, you can be joyful.
- Because God knows sadness, you can cry.
- Because God is eternal, you have a soul that is eternal.
- Because God knows and loves you, it is possible for you to know and love Him (1 John 4:19).

So God created human beings in his image. In the image of God he created them. He created them male and female.

—GENESIS 1:27

How Can I Know for Sure God Loves Me?

God sure is busy. He keeps the stars in the sky and our planet earth spinning in space! You might think He has no time for all His human children. But God is not like us. God is perfect. With His perfect memory, He knows every person's name—including yours! God loves and cares for you a *lot*.

In fact, He knew you even before you were born (Psalm 139:13–16). God even knows exactly how many hairs are on your head! He loves you so much that He watches over you every minute of every day and night—even right now (Psalm 139:1–10).

How else can you know God loves you? The Bible says that even when you can't hear God's voice, He is still watching over and loving you (Psalm 121:4). This is very good news! Sometimes He speaks to you in your heart. Although God is big and strong, His voice is a gentle whisper (1 Kings 19:12). Close your eyes and listen. Can you hear God's voice calling your name? Can you hear Him whispering, *I love you*?

Does God Stop Loving Me When I Sin?

• • • • • • • •

The Bible teaches that sin is what breaks our relationship with God. This is because God is holy. The word *holy* means "set apart by God," who is perfect.

Human beings are not holy. But because God created and loves us, He made a way for our sins to be forgiven. The word *forgive* means "to excuse or pardon." And when God forgives our sins, He also forgets them (Jeremiah 31:34)!

God loves us so much, He sent Jesus to earth to die for our sins (Romans 5:8). Because our sins are forgiven when we believe in Jesus, we can be friends with God. When you sin, you make God very sad—but God never stops loving you.

God's love for you is bigger than any sin.

Know this: there is nothing you can think or say or do that will make God love you any more or any less! But when we do sin, God wants us talk to Him about it. He wants us to admit what we did wrong, say we're sorry, and ask for His forgiveness.

Does God Care What My Body Looks Like?

• • • • • • •

God doesn't care whether your eyes are brown or blue. He doesn't care whether your hair is curly or straight, or whether you wear glasses or use a wheelchair. God creates His children in all shapes, sizes, and colors, and with all kinds of abilities. God makes each of us "in an amazing and wonderful way" (Psalm 139:14). Because He made you special, you are one of a kind! No matter what you look like or how your body works, God loves you just the way you are. God also wants your body and soul to be as healthy as possible (1 Thessalonians 5:23; 3 John verse 2).

I praise you because you made me in an amazing and wonderful way.
—PSALM 139:14

For a healthy body, eat nutritious foods, get enough sleep, and try to get lots of sunshine and exercise. For a healthy soul, read your Bible, talk and listen to God in prayer, go to church, and spend time with friends who love God too. Why are a healthy body and soul important? Because God loves you and wants you to be His special helper, sharing His love with others.

God loves you so much, He wants you to live with Him forever!

In fact, the Bible says God loves you so much that nothing—not even sickness or death—can separate you from His love (Romans 8:38–39). Isn't that amazing?

How Do I Know God Has a Special Purpose for My Life?

• • • • • • • •

When God makes snowflakes, each one is different. Some are big. Some are tiny. Some are star-shaped and pointy. Some are lacy and round. If God makes billions of different snowflakes, think how different He makes each one of His human children!

You are unique. The word *unique* means "one of a kind." You see, there is no one else on earth exactly like you. And God has special work for you to do during your life that only *you* can do. It's the reason you were born.

In fact, God knew and loved you even before you were born (Psalm 139:13–16)! You are God's special child, His "masterpiece," created to be His helper on earth. Your mission in life is to discover the good things God wants you to do. Talk about an exciting adventure!

Here's a hint: the good things God has planned for you to do always have to do with *love*. Why? Because "God is love" (1 John 4:8).

How Can I Get to Know God Better?

• • • • • • •

Here is good news: when it comes to knowing God, kids are natural-born experts! Here are three good ways to get to know God even better:

- Read your Bible. The Bible is God's love letter to you. The more you read it, the more you will get to know and love God.
- Spend time with God in prayer. Prayer is talking and listening to God. Spend time with Him, and you will get to know Him better! Remember: God always has time for you, and when you pray, God always listens.
- Spend time with friends who believe in God. This way you can share what you know about God and pray for one another. You will be amazed how much fun it is!

Do you know what God thinks about you wanting to get to know Him better? It makes Him *so* happy! Why? Because *God loves you* (1 John 3:1).

Is It True That Jesus Knows My Name?

• • • • • • •

Yes, it is true: Jesus knows your name. Jesus knows and loves everything about you, including your name! My favorite Easter story shows how Jesus personally knows and loves each one of us.

Early on Easter morning, Jesus' friend, Mary Magdalene, went to visit His tomb. But the stone was rolled away and Jesus' body wasn't there! There was nothing left but His *grave clothes*, or strips of linen cloth, that they had wrapped Him in.

Mary was *so* upset! How could someone do this? She cried and cried—until she looked into the tomb and saw two angels! "Woman, why are you crying?" they asked. After she told them, she turned around and saw a mysterious man. He, too, asked her why she was so sad. At first, she thought the man was a gardener . . . until He said her name—"*Mary.*" At once she recognized the voice. It was Jesus! He was alive (John 20:10–18)!

Just as Jesus knew Mary's name, He knows your name. You can recognize His voice too.

Jesus knows and loves everything about you.

JESUS

Who Is Jesus?

• • • • • • •

Jesus is God's only Son. He's the most important person who ever lived. Know this: The story of Jesus is not a legend, myth, or fairy tale. It is true. Jesus was a real person. Just like us, Jesus was born, lived, and finally died during His time here on earth. But unlike anyone else ever, three days after He died, Jesus came back to life with a brand-new body designed to live forever. Why? So that one day, after we die, we will get brand-new bodies and live forever with Jesus and God in heaven too!

> **The high priest asked Jesus another question: "Are you the Christ, the Son of the blessed God?" Jesus answered, "I am."**
>
> **—MARK 14:61–62**

One of Jesus' best friends, a man named John, wrote down these words of Jesus: "God loved the world so much that he gave his only Son . . . so that whoever believes in him may not be lost, but have eternal life" (John 3:16).

Oh, there is so much more to learn about Jesus! But this is a good start.

In his gospel, John wrote that Jesus is

the Word (John 1:14)
the Lamb of God (John 1:29, 36)
the Messiah (John 1:41)
the Son of God (John 1:49)
the King of Israel (John 1:49)
the Savior of the world (John 4:42)
the Lord and God (John 20:28)

How Did Jesus Get His Name?

Names had a very special importance in ancient times, especially for the Jewish people. Names were chosen to describe the person. For example, God named the first person in the Bible Adam, from the Hebrew word *adama*, which means both "man" and "earth," or "ground." God did this because Adam was created from "dust from the ground" (Genesis 2:7).

Likewise, Jesus' name has a special meaning. Months before Mary knew she was going to have a baby, an angel visited her. She was very surprised! "You are going to have a son," the angel Gabriel announced. "And His true Father will be God in heaven." He told Mary to name the baby Jesus, which means "savior," or "one who saves the people" (Luke 1:26–35). The angel later appeared to Joseph and told him about the baby Jesus too (Matthew 1:20–21).

It would be many years before Mary and Joseph would really understand why God wanted His only Son to be named Jesus. But because they loved and trusted God, they obeyed Him.

Why Was Jesus Born in a Stable?

• • • • • • •

At the time of Jesus' birth, a Roman emperor named Caesar Augustus ordered that all his people be officially counted in a *census*. To be counted, Mary and Joseph had to travel from their home in Nazareth to Bethlehem. We don't know for certain how Mary and Joseph traveled, but it probably took them about one week by foot. Because Mary was expecting a baby and was probably tired, she might have ridden on a donkey.

> **There were no rooms left in the inn. So [Mary] wrapped the baby with cloths and laid him in a box where animals are fed.**
>
> **—LUKE 2:7**

When Mary and Joseph arrived in Bethlehem, the town was very crowded. There was no room at the village inn. Hospitals hadn't been invented yet, so Mary and Joseph had to stay in a stable.

When Jesus was born, Mary wrapped Him in *swaddling clothes*, or strips of soft cloth, to keep Him snug and warm. Then she gently placed Him in a manger (Luke 2:7). A *manger* is a long, open wooden box or trough that contains hay for cattle and horses to eat.

How happy Mary and Joseph must have been! There is nothing more joyful than welcoming a new baby.

What Was Jesus Like as a Boy?

• • • • • • •

Jesus was very smart and brave. Mary and Joseph raised their Son to be obedient and to love God. When Jesus was twelve years old, He was separated from His parents while visiting the big city of Jerusalem. Three days later, Mary and Joseph found Jesus talking with the grown-up teachers at the temple, and "All who heard [Jesus] were amazed at his understanding and wise answers" (Luke 2:47). Jesus was calm as could be. But His mother was understandably *very* upset. "Son, why did you do this to us?" Mary asked. "Your father and I were very worried about you" (verse 48).

"Why did you have to look for me?" Jesus asked. "You should have known that I must be where my Father's work is!" (verse 49).

Mary and Joseph didn't understand that Jesus was talking about His Father God in heaven. But Jesus wasn't being disrespectful. He was only twelve and just beginning to learn who He really was.

What Did Jesus Look Like?

There were no photographs when Jesus walked and talked on earth, so we don't know for sure what He looked like. But we can guess about several of His physical features.

Because Jesus was from Israel, He probably had dark hair and brown eyes. It is likely that Jesus wore His hair long with a dark, uncut beard. Because Jesus worked as a carpenter, He probably had strong, muscular arms (Mark 6:3). Because people liked to be with Jesus, we can assume He laughed and smiled a lot. Because Jesus loved people, He must have had very kind eyes.

Why Is Jesus So Important?

• • • • • • •

Jesus is not just any human being. Jesus is the most important person who ever lived in the history of our world. Jesus said that He is God's very own Son (Mark 14:61–62).

Jesus was so close to God that when He prayed, or talked to God, He called God "Abba" (Mark 14:36). In Jesus' native Aramaic language, the word *abba* means "daddy" or "papa." Imagine that!

Jesus was so close to God that He said, "I and the Father are one" (John 10:30 NIV). Jesus is different from all other leaders of a religion who ever lived because three days after He died, He was raised from the dead and received a new body designed to live forever.

Jesus is alive today with His Father in heaven. He is alive in our hearts through God's Holy Spirit.

Because Jesus is alive, He knows and loves you—and you can know and love Him.

This is very good news!

Jesus is different from all other religious leaders because He was raised from the dead.

What Is the Temptation of Christ?

• • • • • • •

Because Jesus was human, He was tempted. We call the most famous episode of Jesus being tempted the "Temptation of Christ" (Matthew 4:1–11; Mark 1:12–13; Luke 4:1–13).

God's Holy Spirit led Jesus into the desert to *fast*, or to not eat food, for forty days. Then the devil, known as Satan, tried to tempt Jesus to turn stones into bread. Jesus said, "A person does not live only by eating bread. But a person lives by everything the Lord says" (Matthew 4:4). Then Satan tried again. If Jesus was God, why not jump off the highest tower in Jerusalem and see if the angels would catch Him? Jesus said, "Do not test the Lord your God" (verse 7). Then Satan showed Jesus all the kingdoms of the world, saying that if Jesus would only worship him, He could have everything! Jesus said, "Go away from me, Satan!" (verse 10).

> **While [Jesus] was in the desert, he was tempted by Satan. Then angels came and took care of Jesus.**
>
> —MARK 1:13

No matter how much He was tempted, Jesus would worship only God. Jesus didn't live for money, fame, or power. Jesus lived to show the world how much God loves us.

What Is the Transfiguration of Christ?

• • • • • • •

One day Jesus took His disciples Peter, James, and John up on a high mountain. Suddenly Jesus' clothes became glistening white. His face shone like the sun. The Bible says that Jesus was *transfigured*, or changed. It was amazing!

At the same time, two famous Jewish prophets from the Old Testament, Elijah and Moses, miraculously appeared, even though they lived on earth hundreds of years before!

Suddenly, a bright cloud covered them, and God's voice said, "This is my Son, whom I love; with him I am well pleased. Listen to him!" (Matthew 17:5 NIV). When the disciples heard this, they fell on their faces, terrified. Jesus comforted them, saying, "Get up. Don't be afraid" (Matthew 17:7 NIV). When they looked up, Elijah and Moses were gone. Jesus told them to wait until He had been raised from the dead before telling anyone what they had seen (Matthew 17:1–9; Mark 9:2–10; Luke 9:28–36).

As you can imagine, the event made a *big* impression on Peter, James, and John! Later, Peter wrote a firsthand account all about it (2 Peter 1:16–18).

Did Jesus Ever Do Anything Wrong?

• • • • • • •

We know from the Bible that Jesus was tempted like any other human. But because Jesus is God's Son, He never gave in to temptation. He never did anything wrong in God's eyes. Not once!

To be tempted is very stressful. When you are tempted, you feel like a giant magnet is pulling you to give in and think, say, or do something that deep down inside you know is wrong.

Jesus was fully human, so He knows what it feels like to be tempted. At the same time, Jesus said, "He who has seen me has seen the Father" (John 14:9). By this, Jesus meant that He and God are one and the same.

When Jesus was tempted to do wrong, He prayed and asked God to help Him. Jesus loved and trusted God, and God answered His prayers. Because Jesus suffered when He was tempted, He understands and is able to help us when we are tempted too (Hebrews 2:18).

Jesus never sinned.

Not even once.

Why Did Jesus Do Miracles?

A *miracle* is something wonderful that cannot be explained by natural or scientific laws. Miracles are from our good and loving God. Miracles are not magic. Miracles are real.

Jesus did loving, kindhearted miracles. He made many sick people well (Mark 5:21–42). He made lame people walk (John 5:2–9). He made blind people see (Matthew 9:27–30). He made deaf people hear (Mark 7:31–37). He even brought His friend Lazarus, who had died, back to life (John 11:1–44)! In fact, the Bible records at least thirty-seven detailed, true, eyewitnessed miracles of Jesus. His friend John said there were more: "If every one of them were written down, I think the whole world would not be big enough for all the books that would be written" (John 21:25).

Remember: Jesus did not do miracles for money or to show off. Jesus did miracles so people would believe that He is God's Son, and to show how much God loves and cares for His children—including *you*!

Can Anyone Believe in Jesus?

• • • • • • • •

Yes, anyone can believe in Jesus. God loves all His children and wants them all to believe in Him and in His Son, Jesus.

But God does not force His children to love Him. It is up to every person, each on their own, to have faith in His Son, Jesus.

There is an old saying that "Jesus is a gentleman." That is, Jesus will not force His way into your heart. Instead, the Bible says, He stands at the door and knocks (Revelation 3:20). He enters and lives in your heart when He is invited.

The good news is that it's never too late to believe in God and in His Son, Jesus. You can be ten years old or one hundred years old. God is very patient and forgiving. God is always waiting with open arms for His children to come to Him (Luke 15:11–20).

How Can I Get to Know Jesus?

• • • • • • •

The best way to get to know Jesus is to talk to Him. Tell Him that you want to get to know Him better. Jesus is always eager and ready to hear your prayers.

Just pray: "Jesus, I really want to know You. I believe You are the Son of God. I believe that You died on the cross for my sins. Thank You for loving me so much. Now please come into my heart and live in me."

When Jesus lives in your heart, He will help you tell right from wrong. He'll forgive you when you make mistakes (1 John 1:9). He'll comfort you when you're feeling down. He'll be your very best friend—the best you ever had (John 15:15)!

How can you be sure Jesus will come into your heart if you ask Him? Because Jesus said He would, and He always, always keeps His promises (1 Thessalonians 5:24; Hebrews 10:23).

Why does Jesus want to do all this for you? Because Jesus loves you.

Jesus wants to be your very best friend.

JESUS' DEATH AND RESURRECTION

What Is the Passion of Christ?

• • • • • • •

The word *passion* comes from an old Latin word that means "suffering" or "enduring." For Christians, the Passion of Christ refers to the final days in Jesus' life, beginning when He rode into Jerusalem on a donkey and ending with His crucifixion and death on the cross.

During Holy Week, many Christian churches read the Passion story from the Bible aloud, in a dramatic fashion, with church leaders and members taking part. Reading the Passion story this way can bring the story to life and be a very moving experience.

In the Bible, there are four versions of the Passion of Christ, each with different details. Here is where you can find them in your Bible:

- Matthew 21:1–11, 26:1–27:66
- Mark 11:1–11, 14:1–15:47
- Luke 19:28–40, 22:1–23:56
- John 12:12–19, 18:1–19:42

You don't have to be in church to read the Passion stories aloud. You can read these true, amazing stories any time of the year, on your own or with family and friends.

What Is the Last Supper?

• • • • • • •

On the night before Jesus died, He shared a special Passover meal with His disciples. Today we call this meal the Last Supper (Luke 22:7–30). Jesus knew He was going to die. To show the disciples how much He loved them, Jesus washed their feet (John 13:1–17).

> **"I, your Lord and Teacher, have washed your feet. So you also should wash each other's feet."**
>
> **—JOHN 13:14**

This was shocking! The roads in Israel were dusty and dirty. So were the disciples' feet. Jesus was their *rabbi*, or teacher. In Jesus' day, to wash his students' dirty feet is something a rabbi would *never* do! But Jesus saw things differently.

This was Jesus' way of saying that no one is greater than anyone else, and that they (and we!) should lovingly and humbly serve each other.

During Holy Week, on the Thursday before Easter, many churches remember this event with a special Holy Thursday service where the church leaders and members wash each other's feet, just as Jesus did with His disciples.

What Did Judas Iscariot Do That Was So Bad?

Judas Iscariot was one of Jesus' twelve original apostles. Judas was looking for a powerful earthly king for God's people. But Jesus came to tell the world about the kingdom of God. Judas was bitterly disappointed.

Judas's heart turned evil. Late one night, Judas led a crowd of priests and soldiers to Jesus and His disciples. Judas had told them that he would let them know who Jesus was by giving Him a kiss. But Jesus knew all along that Judas would betray Him (John 6:64, 70–71). And here is the truly awful part: Immediately, after betraying Jesus, Judas knew he had made a terrible mistake. He tried to give the money back to the priests, but it was too late. Judas felt so guilty that he hanged himself (Matthew 27:3–10). Because of Judas's betrayal, Jesus died on the cross. But here is good news: Because of Jesus' death, our sins are forgiven. Because Jesus was raised from the dead, one day we will be too.

Who Is Pontius Pilate, and What Makes Him So Important?

• • • • • • •

Pontius Pilate was the Roman governor in charge of Judea from AD 26 to 36. After the priests and soldiers arrested Jesus, they brought Him to Pontius Pilate for sentencing. But Pilate sensed in his heart that Jesus had done nothing wrong. A criminal named Barabbas was also waiting to be sentenced. Because it was the Jewish festival of Passover, one criminal could be let go. Pontius Pilate couldn't make up his mind. He asked the crowd: "Whom shall I set free? Jesus or Barabbas?"

"Barabbas!"

"But what about Jesus?"

"Crucify Him!" the crowd roared (Matthew 27:15–23, paraphrase).

Pontius Pilate was not happy, but he handed Jesus over. He showed his displeasure by washing his hands and saying, "I am not guilty of this man's death" (verse 24). Pilate reminds us that the story of Jesus is real. Pontius Pilate was a historical person. So is Jesus. This is very good news!

Did Jesus Know He Was Going to Die?

Several times Jesus told His disciples that He was going to die. But each time He mentioned His death, the disciples cried, "No! Don't say such a thing!" Such talk made them very sad. Jesus also told His disciples that three days after His death, He was going to rise from the dead and overcome death forever (Matthew 17:22–23). Because no one had ever risen from the dead this way, this was impossible for the disciples to understand. It didn't make sense. In fact, it was so strange that the disciples were afraid to ask Jesus about it (Mark 9:32)!

Jesus told His disciples ahead of time about His death and resurrection for a special reason: so when these things happened, the disciples would remember His words, and they would believe (Luke 24:8).

Why Was Jesus Killed?

• • • • • • •

Many people understood and believed that Jesus truly was God's Son. They witnessed Jesus' love, forgiveness, and healing miracles. They liked what Jesus taught about God's great love for His children. But many other people did not.

Some people thought Jesus was crazy.

Others thought Jesus was lying.

Still others said it was against the law for Jesus to say that God was His Father (John 10:36).

So when Jesus was still a young man, just thirty-three years old, He was killed. Jesus was *crucified*, or put to death by hanging on a wooden cross on a sad, lonely hill called *Golgotha*, or "the Place of the Skull" (John 19:17). The word *crucify* means "to attach to a cross." It was a terrible, painful way to die.

Jesus was killed by fearful, angry people who couldn't find it in their hearts to have faith in Him and in His Father God.

What Is the Resurrection of Jesus?

• • • • • • •

Three days after Jesus died, early in the morning, His friend Mary Magdalene and some other women went to visit the tomb where Jesus' body had been laid. But when they arrived, the big stone that covered the opening to the tomb had been rolled away. And that wasn't all.

The tomb was empty! *Who took the body of our dear Jesus?* the women wondered. Moments later, they made a wonderful, important, extraordinary discovery: Jesus was alive! He had *come back to life*!

The word *resurrect* means "to bring back to life."

The angel said to the women, "Don't be afraid. I know that you are looking for Jesus, the one who was killed on the cross. But he is not here. He has risen from death as he said he would."

—MATTHEW 28:5-6

So, as fast as their legs could carry them, the women ran to tell the disciples the good news.

Each of the four Gospels reports different, exciting eyewitness details about Jesus' resurrection, which is the most important event in human history! To get the full story, read all four Gospel reports (Matthew 28:1–10; Mark 16:1–8; Luke 24:1–12; John 20:1–18).

Why Is Jesus' Resurrection So Important?

• • • • • • •

After Jesus' resurrection, He explained that soon He would be going back to heaven. But before He left, He had some very good news.

> **Jesus said to her, "I am the resurrection and the life. He who believes in me will have life even if he dies."**
>
> **—JOHN 11:25**

"The good news," said Jesus, "is that because I have come back to life, you can too. After you die, you can live forever with My Father God and Me in heaven. God loves you so much, He wants this for you. God wants you to believe in Him and Me. God wants to forgive your sins. God wants you to live in His kingdom forever" (John 3:16, paraphrased).

What a happy place God's kingdom is! That's because everyone in heaven is happy and healthy. Everyone in heaven has new bodies that live forever, and there is no more death or sadness or crying or pain (Revelation 21:4).

Jesus' resurrection means our sins can be forgiven.

If you believe in Jesus, you can live forever with God and Jesus in heaven. This is very good news!

How Can I Know for Sure That Jesus Was Resurrected?

• • • • • • •

Know this: The resurrection of Jesus is not a legend, myth, or fairy tale. It's a true, historical fact. It is also at the very heart of our Christian faith. Jesus lived on earth in His resurrected body for about forty days. He appeared to eyewitnesses ten times:

1. The first people to see the resurrected Jesus were His friend Mary Magdalene and other women (Matthew 28:1–9).
2. Jesus appeared to two disciples walking on the road (Mark 16:12). At first they didn't recognize Jesus. Later, while eating with Jesus, they did. Then Jesus disappeared (Luke 24:13–31).
3. Jesus appeared to Peter in Jerusalem (Luke 24:34).
4. Jesus appeared to a group of disciples, excluding Thomas, in the upper room in Jerusalem (John 20:19). Even though the doors were locked, Jesus appeared.
5. A week after Jesus first appeared to the disciples, He suddenly appeared *again* in the upper room. This time Thomas saw Jesus with his own eyes, and he believed (John 20:24–29)!

6. Jesus appeared to seven disciples at the Sea of Galilee (John 21:1–4).
7. Jesus appeared to the eleven disciples on a mountain in Galilee (Matthew 28:16–20).
8. Jesus appeared to five hundred other eyewitnesses (1 Corinthians 15:6).
9. Jesus appeared to the disciple James (1 Corinthians 15:7).
10. Jesus appeared to all those who witnessed His ascension into heaven (Mark 16:19).

What Is the Ascension of Christ?

• • • • • • •

Jesus walked and talked on earth in His resurrected body for about forty days. Then He gathered His disciples on the Mount of Olives. It was time for Jesus to join His Father God in heaven. Before Jesus left, He told the disciples to preach the good news of God's love everywhere. He also told them to stay in Jerusalem until the Holy Spirit came to them. Suddenly, to everyone's amazement, Jesus was "taken up into heaven" (Mark 16:19 NIV).

The word *ascension* means "the act of going up."

Witnesses said it was as though a cloud took Jesus from the disciples' sight (Acts 1:8–9). Then Jesus was "taken up into heaven."

Many Christians celebrate this historic event with a special Ascension Day service, thirty-nine days after Easter Sunday. At the service they read aloud the Bible story of Jesus' return to heaven. The Bible says Jesus will one day return to earth "in the same way" He left (Acts 1:10–11). What an exciting day that will be!

After the Lord Jesus said these things to the followers, he was carried up into heaven. There, Jesus sat at the right side of God.

—MARK 16:19

What Is the Second Coming of Christ?

While the disciples were gazing up in wonder at Jesus' ascension into heaven, two angels in white robes appeared. "Men of Galilee," they said, "why are you standing here looking into the sky? You saw Jesus taken away from you into heaven. He will come back in the same way you saw him go" (Acts 1:10–11).

> **"Then people will see the Son of Man coming in clouds with great power and glory."**
> **—MARK 13:26**

Jesus will return to earth again someday. When Jesus comes back, everyone will recognize that He is God's Son. There will be no confusion or mistaking His identity. The Bible says that Jesus will come "in clouds" with God's holy angels (Mark 13:26). For people who believe in Jesus, this will be the happiest day in human history (Hebrews 9:28). Jesus will gather us all in His big, strong arms, and our hearts will be filled with joy like we've never known!

This big event has become known as the second coming of Christ.

This promise of Jesus' return to earth is so important that early Christians greeted one another with the Aramaic language word "*Maranatha!*" which means "The Lord is coming" or "Come, oh, Lord!"

No one knows for sure when Jesus will return to earth. Not even the angels. In fact, Jesus says that only His Father God in heaven knows for sure (Mark 13:32–37)!

How then should we prepare for the second coming of Jesus? Jesus answered this key question with two words: "Be ready!" (Mark 13:37). While we watch and wait, Jesus wants us to live our lives as though He were coming back today. That's because He can come at any time. He could come this very hour. He could come before you finish reading this sentence. The important thing is that He wants us to be ready for His arrival. What can we do to be ready for Jesus? Love God and love each other. Love is the key. Here is what we do know for sure: Jesus promises He will return—and Jesus always keeps His promises (Deuteronomy 7:9).

How do we know for sure that Jesus will return?

Because Jesus always keeps His promises (Deuteronomy 7:9; 1 Corinthians 1:9).

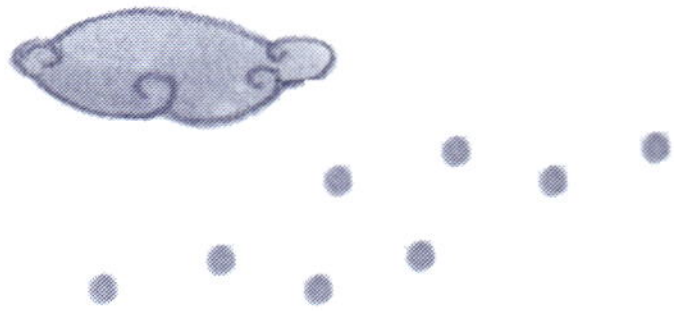

THE HOLY SPIRIT

Who Is the Holy Spirit?

Did you notice that this question does *not* begin with "*What*," but rather "*Who*" is the Holy Spirit? This is because the Holy Spirit is not just a vague, floaty idea. The Holy Spirit is a powerful, living Person!

As Christians, we understand God to be made up of three living Persons: God the Father; God's Son, Jesus; and God's Holy Spirit. We call this the Holy Trinity. The Holy Spirit is the third person of the Holy Trinity. But the Holy Spirit is no less important! Like God and Jesus, the Holy Spirit *is* love.

In the Old Testament, God's Holy Spirit was known as the giver of life, and as the One who spoke God's Word through the prophets. In the New Testament, the Holy Spirit is described as God's love poured into our hearts (Romans 5:5). The Holy Spirit is the way God lives in the hearts of human beings—the way God lives in *your* heart!

The Holy Spirit helps us grow to be more like Jesus and opens our minds to understanding God's Word in the Bible. The Holy Spirit allows God to use our lives to accomplish His work on earth.

How loving God is to fill us with His Holy Spirit!

The Holy Spirit helps us grow to be more like Jesus.

How Does the Holy Spirit Help Me?

• • • • • • •

The Holy Spirit gives you God's special power to love (Romans 5:5).

The Holy Spirit is like a battery in a flashlight. Without a battery, a flashlight looks just fine on the outside. But when it's dark and you need to use it, it is of no help.

A flashlight *with* a battery looks the same on the outside as the flashlight without a battery. But when it's dark and you need to use it, it works. It shines the light into the darkness and keeps you from stumbling.

God's Holy Spirit living in your heart is like your spiritual battery.

Another name used for God's Holy Spirit is "the Helper." That's because the Holy Spirit helps you in many ways. He gives you the power to tell right from wrong, to care more about other people, and to think, speak, and act more like Jesus. He gives you special gifts from God. God's Holy Spirit gives you the power to shine the light of God's love in a world that can sometimes be dark and scary. Whatever the situation, you can always count on God's Holy Spirit to help you.

What Is the Fruit of the Holy Spirit?

• • • • • • •

When God's Holy Spirit lives in your heart, others can tell. That's because over time, the Holy Spirit *transforms* or changes you. The Holy Spirit produces outward, visible signs that He's living in you and helping you be more like Jesus.

These signs of the Holy Spirit are sometimes called "fruit." They are called fruit because fruit is an outward sign of a healthy, living plant. Fruit is beautiful to look at. Fruit is delicious to eat. Fruit nourishes the body. The fruit that the Holy Spirit produces is an outward sign of a healthy soul.

The fruit of the Spirit is love, joy, peace, patience, kindness, goodness, faithfulness, gentleness, self-control.

—GALATIANS 5:22–23 ESV

What is the fruit of the Holy Spirit? It's all the wonderful, loving qualities that God has planted and are growing in your heart: love, joy, peace, patience, kindness, goodness, faithfulness, gentleness, and self-control.

THE BIBLE

What Is the Bible?

The Bible is the most important book in the world. Why? Because the Bible is the true, living Holy Word of God.

The apostle Paul described the Bible as *inspired*, or "God-breathed" (2 Timothy 3:16 NIV). God breathed through the hearts and minds of the human beings who wrote the Bible. That makes the Bible different from all other books.

When you pick up a Bible, you are actually holding a whole library! That's because the Bible contains sixty-six books, written by forty different people, over a period of about two thousand years. Sometimes the Bible is referred to as *Scripture*, which means "holy writings."

All Scripture is inspired by God.
—2 TIMOTHY 3:16

In the Bible you will discover an awesome collection of real, true-life stories about kings and queens, angels and prophets, adventure and love, plus poetry, songs, prayers, and letters—even predictions about the future! Best of all, you will read the real, true-life story of Jesus, God's only Son, sent to earth to save the world. Talk about exciting!

Remember: The Bible is not a dry, boring book. It is the living Word of God.

The Bible is God's special love letter to you!

How Did We Get the Bible?

• • • • • • •

The Bible begins with the oldest stories about how God created the universe. In ancient times, most people didn't know how to read or write, so they passed these stories down *orally*, or by mouth. Parents told their children, who told their children, and so on. Over time, people wrote the stories down—first on papyrus scrolls, later on parchment.

> **"Get a scroll. Write on it all the words I have spoken to you."**
> **—JEREMIAH 36:2**

In the early Christian church, people who loved God had *councils*, or special meetings, to decide which books would be included in the Bible. They prayed for God's Holy Spirit to help them choose. In the fifteenth century, the mechanical printing press was invented by a man named Johannes Gutenberg in Germany. In 1457, Gutenberg's Bible was the very first complete book ever printed. It was printed in two huge volumes of 1,282 unnumbered pages!

Over the years, billions of Bibles have been printed. It's the world's best-selling book and has been translated into more than two thousand languages.

Thanks to the Bible, people everywhere can learn about God's great love!

How Did the Bible Get Its Name?

• • • • • • •

In what is now the country of Lebanon, the Phoenician city of Gebal was once a busy Mediterranean seaport. In Bible times, the Greek name for Gebal was *Byblos*. *Byblos* was also the Greek word for *papyrus*, the grassy reed from which the earliest form of paper was made. Maybe this is because trading paper was big business in Byblos, or maybe it's because that's where papyrus grew. No one knows for sure.

At any rate, the word *byblos*, or papyrus, gives us the Greek word *biblios*, which means "books." Papyrus is the kind of paper the scribes used for writing the books of the Bible. In ancient times, the only people able to read and write were called *scribes*, which comes from the Latin word that means "to write."

Today the English word *Bible* literally means "The Book."

Here's a fun fact: the word *Bible* is not found in the Bible! This is because the term didn't come into use until long after all the books of the Bible were completed and chosen.

How Do I Know the Bible Is True?

• • • • • • • •

The Bible is different from every other book in the world. Why? Because it was written by many different people who wrote under the inspiration of God. Through His Holy Spirit, God *breathed His truth into the hearts and minds of the writers.* God inspired the writers so they would know just what to write. God's Holy Spirit is alive today in the pages of every Bible! The Bible speaks God's truth to our hearts. This is why it's often called "God's Word." The Bible has the power to speak God's truth to *you*!

Here is an important and interesting fact: the Bible is the *most documented and reliable book* in the world. Scholars of the Bible have more than *thirteen thousand* ancient copies of portions of the New Testament, which they continue to study and learn from to this very day! New discoveries by biblical archaeologists also help prove that events in the Bible really happened. An *archaeologist* is a scientist who studies human history by digging up artifacts and remains. Isn't that amazing?

The Bible is the most reliable book in the world.

What Is the Difference Between the Old Testament and the New Testament?

• • • • • • •

The books of the Bible are divided into two sections: the Old Testament and the New Testament. The word *testament* means "covenant," which means "a promise or agreement." In the Bible, the covenant is between God and His children, which includes *you*!

The Old Testament starts before the beginning of time and covers thousands of years. It's more than twice as long as the New Testament. In it, we learn about God's love for the Jews, the people of Israel. God made a covenant with His people (Genesis 13:14–17) and expected them to believe in Him, love Him, and obey His laws. This was not always easy!

The New Testament begins with the birth of God's Son, Jesus (Matthew 1:18–25). The books of Matthew, Mark, Luke, John, and Acts tell the story of Jesus. Acts also tells about the exciting arrival of God's Holy Spirit on earth, and about the birth and growth of the early church. Many books in the New Testament are letters from people who personally knew Jesus on earth. The last book, Revelation, is what God told the apostle John in a vision about the future.

In the New Testament, God makes a new *covenant*, or agreement, with His people. Through believing in His Son, Jesus, God invites everyone to become one of His children—including you (Romans 8:14)!

Most of the Old Testament was written in Hebrew, the language of Israel, or Aramaic, a language similar to Hebrew. The books of the New Testament were originally written in Greek. The Old and New Testaments are separated in history by about four hundred years! If you like, open your Bible and turn to the table of contents to see for yourself the thirty-nine books of the Old Testament and the twenty-seven books of the New Testament. God's Word is right at your fingertips!

What Is the Difference Between a Jew and a Gentile?

• • • • • • •

The word *Jew* is the most commonly used name for the people of Israel (Jeremiah 32:12). It is derived from the Hebrew word *Yehudi*, meaning "one who comes from Judea." Judea was the ancient region of southern Palestine that was made up of modern-day southern Israel and southwest Jordan. Jews are also sometimes called Israelites or Hebrews.

A Gentile is any person who is not Jewish. Today there are many Gentiles who love God very much!

Which Bible Is Right for Me?

• • • • • • •

Some Bibles have colorful pictures and maps. Others have study guides and notes. Some Bibles use literal translations straight from the original Hebrew and Greek manuscripts. Others use modern language. Some Bibles are bound in leather and trimmed with gold. Others are paperback. Some Bibles can be read as e-books on your computer or phone!

The best way to discover which Bible is right for you is to visit your church library or local bookstore and look at different Bibles. Hold the Bible in your hands. Open it up. Flip through the pages. Read a few passages. You need a Bible you can understand. God wants you to understand how much He loves you!

If you can't afford to buy a Bible, talk to your pastor, youth minister, or other trusted grown-up who loves Jesus. Tell him or her that you would very much like to have your own Bible. God wants all His children to have a Bible. And that includes *you*!

You need a Bible you can understand.

What Are Some Tips for Reading My Bible?

• • • • • • •

The Bible is not just any book. It's the true, inspired Holy Word of God! Because the Bible is the living Word of God, when you read your Bible, God can actually speak to you! Isn't that amazing? The next time you open your Bible, try these helpful tips:

- Before you start reading, take a moment to pray. Ask God to open your mind and heart to understand His Word and to hear His voice.
- Ask yourself, "What kind of book is this?" Remember, the Bible is actually a library of different kinds of books!
- Read a short section of the Bible carefully. Think deeply about what the words mean.
- Ask yourself, "What is God trying to say to me right now?"
- Decide how you can act on what you've learned. For example, if the Bible passage you read is about showing love to others, ask God if there is someone special He wants you to love with a kind word or action.

How Do I Memorize Bible Verses?

• • • • • • •

Memorizing Bible verses is easier than you may think. Because everyone learns differently, there are no "right" or "wrong" ways to memorize Bible verses. Here are a few helpful hints!

- **Listen** as someone else reads a Bible verse to you, or record yourself reading the verse and listen to it several times. Keep listening to it until you have the verse memorized.
- **Read** the Bible verse to yourself over and over, out loud or silently, until you can say it out loud by memory.
- **Write** the Bible verse ten times. When you think you have the verse memorized, say it out loud.
- **Sing!** If the verse is short, make up a little tune to go with the words. Sing it over and over until you remember it.
- **Imagine** a story or pictures in your mind that will help you remember the verse.
- **Memorize** with a friend or family member. Encourage each other as you see which methods work best for each of you.

PEOPLE IN THE BIBLE

Who Are Adam and Eve?

• • • • • • •

The Bible says God created the first man, Adam, from the earth. But God recognized that Adam was lonely, so He created the first woman, Eve (Genesis 2:18, 3:20). They lived happily on earth in a beautiful garden called Eden. God loved them dearly, and they loved and trusted God back.

God gave Adam and Eve everything they needed for a healthy, happy life. He had only one rule: do not eat the fruit from the tree of the "knowledge of good and evil" (Genesis 2:17), because if they ate its fruit, they would die! For a while, Adam and Eve obeyed.

But one day Eve came across a tricky *serpent*, or snake. "Why do you listen to God?" the serpent hissed. "He doesn't really care about you. Eat the fruit and you'll be fine," he lied. At that moment, Eve forgot all about loving and trusting God. She believed the serpent and ate the fruit. Then she shared it with Adam. At once, just as God had warned, sin and death entered God's beautiful world. Adam and Eve made a big mistake when they ate the forbidden fruit!

Knowing they had disobeyed, God came looking for His children in the cool breeze of the early evening. "Where are you?" He called. But Adam and Eve were nowhere to be found. They were hiding. For the first time, they felt the sickening pain of shame. Guilt. Anger. Betrayal. Hopelessness. Fear. For the first time, they felt the pain of separation from each other and—worst of all—from their beloved Father God. Oh, what a dark day for the world!

Over the years, people have called the story of how sin came into the world "the fall of man" or "the fall." But here is good news: Even though Adam and Eve sinned, God never stopped loving them. Likewise, even when we sin, God never stops loving us. He loves us so much that He sent His only Son, Jesus, to earth to overcome sin and death!

Who Is Abraham?

• • • • • • •

Abraham is the first patriarch (*pay*-tree-ark) of the Jewish people. The word *patriarch* means "father." He is one of our spiritual forefathers too!

Abraham was born in the ancient city of Ur in what is now Iraq. He was given the name *Abram*, which means "exalted father" (Genesis 11:27–28). Back then, people believed in many *deities*, or false gods. Abram's father, Terah, was, according to tradition, an idol merchant.

Not much is known about Abram's childhood, but over the years he stopped believing in his father's idols. Over time, Abram came to believe in the one true Creator, Father God. Back then, this was remarkable, and it made God *very* happy.

> **Abram believed the Lord. And the Lord accepted Abram's faith, and that faith made him right with God.**
>
> —GENESIS 15:6

Because of Abram's great, unshakeable faith, God said to him, "I am changing your name from Abram to Abraham. . . . I am making you a father of many nations" (Genesis 17:5). The name *Abraham* means "father of many." The Bible says Abraham "died at a good old age" (Genesis 25:8 NIV) and was buried with his beloved wife, Sarah. He was 175 years old (Genesis 25:7)!

Who Is Sarah?

• • • • • • •

Sarah was Abraham's wife. When Sarah and Abraham were married, she was known as *Sarai*, which means "quarrelsome." Before the birth of her son, Isaac, God changed her name to *Sarah*, which means "princess" or "noblewoman." Just as God chose Abraham to become the *patriarch*, or father of the Jewish people, He chose Sarah to become the *matriarch*, or mother.

Sarah was beautiful. She was also unable to have children (Genesis 11:30). This made Sarah very sad. It also made God's promise of a son seem impossible!

When Sarah was ninety and Abraham was almost one hundred years old, three strangers came to visit them at their tent. Sent by God, they were actually angels with a very important message: "About this time a year from now . . . Sarah will have a son" (Genesis 18:10). Can you imagine? Sarah laughed because she thought this was impossible. But nothing's impossible with God! She gave birth to a son and named him *Isaac*, which means "laughter." Isn't that amazing?

Sarah died at 127 years of age (Genesis 23:1). She's the only woman in the Bible whose age is given, and she was buried with Abraham in the promised land (Genesis 23:19).

Who Is Isaac?

• • • • • • •

Isaac was the only beloved son of Abraham and his wife, Sarah. His birth was a miracle, because his mother was ninety years old when she had him! Isaac is the second *patriarch*, or father, of the Jewish people.

Like his father, Isaac loved and trusted God. But he was about to be part of a very hard test. In Isaac's day, when faithful people worshiped God, they often sacrificed an animal. The word *sacrifice* comes from a Latin word that means "holy." The sacrificed animal was usually a goat, ram, lamb, or calf. First it was killed, then put on a fire and cooked as a "burnt offering." Meat was valuable, and the animal was considered a gift to God.

One day, when Isaac was still a boy, God commanded Abraham to take his only beloved son and offer him as a sacrifice (Genesis 22:1–2). How could this be?

Although Abraham must have been scared and confused, he did not argue. He loved and trusted God. Abraham went up the mountain with Isaac. On their way up, Isaac asked where the animal to be sacrificed was. Abraham said, "God will give us the lamb." At a certain spot they stopped, and Abraham built an *altar*, or platform. Then he tied up Isaac to sacrifice him! Suddenly an angel called out: "Stop! Let him go!" There in a thicket of bushes, trapped by his horns, was a ram. God had provided a perfect sacrifice. Because Abraham was obedient, God blessed him *and* Isaac for generations (Genesis 22)! This is a story of amazing trust.

Isaac was about thirty-seven years old when his mother, Sarah, died. Isaac loved his mother dearly and grieved her loss. Abraham sent his servant to find heartbroken Isaac a good wife.

He returned with the beautiful Rebekah. Isaac loved Rebekah, and she comforted him in his sorrow. The Bible says that Isaac, like his father Abraham, lived a long life and was 180 years old when he died (Genesis 35:28–29).

Abraham's willingness to sacrifice his only beloved son, Isaac, is similar in many surprising ways to God's sacrifice of His Son, Jesus, even though these two events happened hundreds of years apart. Here are more amazing ways Isaac and Jesus are alike:

- They were the beloved sons of their fathers (Isaac: Genesis 22:2; Jesus: John 3:16).
- They were named and their births foretold by God (Isaac: Genesis 17:19; Jesus: Matthew 1:21).
- They were born miraculously (Isaac: Genesis 21:1–3; Jesus: Luke 1:34–35).
- They obeyed the will of their fathers, even if it was *very* difficult (Isaac: Genesis 22:9–10; Jesus: Philippians 2:8).
- They were saved by God in totally unexpected, surprising ways (Isaac: Genesis 22:10–14; Jesus: Matthew 28:2–5).
- They both fulfilled important promises by God that would change the course of world and human history (Isaac: Genesis 12:3; Jesus: Acts 13:23).

Isn't that amazing?

Who Is Jacob?

• • • • • • •

Jacob was the second-born twin son of Isaac and Rebekah. Even in his mother's womb, Jacob struggled with his brother, Esau (Genesis 25:22). The name *Jacob* means "holder of the heel" or "one who overthrows." Jacob is the third and final *patriarch*, or father, of the Jewish people.

Jacob and Esau did not get along. The firstborn Esau was his father's favorite, and Jacob was Rebekah's favorite. In Bible days, firstborn sons received an *inheritance*, or special gift. Esau didn't understand how valuable his inheritance was, but Jacob did. And he plotted to take advantage of Esau.

One day Jacob made a pot of soup. Esau came in hungry from hunting all day and asked for a delicious bowlful. Jacob said sure—as long as Esau would trade him his inheritance. Esau was so hungry that he agreed (Genesis 25:29–34)!

Years later, Jacob also tricked his father into giving him an important firstborn blessing meant for Esau. When Esau found out, he was so angry that he wanted to kill Jacob! So Jacob fled to a faraway land (Genesis 27:1–45).

Years passed. Jacob had his own family and desperately wanted to return home. He missed his mother and father. He even missed Esau! When God told Jacob to go home in a dream, Jacob was happy to obey. There was only one problem: Esau. How would his angry brother react? Jacob asked for God's protection (Genesis 32:9–12).

The night before Jacob's meeting with Esau, a mysterious man unexpectedly showed up and demanded that Jacob wrestle with him. All night long, the two men fought. The man hurt Jacob's hip, but Jacob still wouldn't give up. "I won't let you go until you bless me," Jacob demanded. Before blessing Jacob, the man did something very strange. He gave Jacob a new name, *Israel*, which means "he struggles with God."

It turned out the "man" was actually God (Genesis 32:26–28)! When Jacob finally met up with Esau, all was forgiven and the brothers hugged and cried (Genesis 33:4). Isn't that beautiful? Jacob lived to be 147 (Genesis 47:28). Before Jacob died, he blessed all his sons, who would go on to become the heads of the twelve tribes of Israel (Genesis 49:1–28).

Who Is Joseph?

• • • • • • •

Joseph was the eleventh of Jacob's twelve sons. The name *Joseph* means "God increases." Because Joseph was his father's favorite, his ten older brothers resented him. Once Jacob gave Joseph a beautiful, fancy coat. His brothers were furious! They were also jealous that Joseph had the supernatural gift of prophecy and could interpret dreams. When Joseph told them that he dreamed he would one day rule over them, they were so angry that they plotted to kill him!

One day, when they were working out in the fields, the brothers grabbed Joseph, took his coat, and threw him into a deep pit. At the last minute, instead of killing him, they decided to sell him as a slave to Ishmaelite traders. As the traders' caravan pulled away, Joseph's brothers smeared his coat with goat's blood. They showed the bloody coat to their father and lied, saying Joseph had been killed by wild animals. Jacob was devastated.

Joseph was only seventeen when he was sold into slavery in Egypt. His new owner was an Egyptian official, Potiphar. Potiphar's wife tried to flirt with Joseph, but when he rejected her, she had him thrown into jail!

Still, Joseph never lost his faith in God.

In jail, he interpreted dreams for his fellow prisoners (Genesis 40). Word of his gift got back to Egypt's *Pharaoh* (*fare*-oh), or king, who'd been having upsetting dreams. Pharaoh called Joseph to his palace. Joseph told Pharaoh that his dreams were God's warning that Egypt would have seven years of good harvests, but then seven terrible years of famine (Genesis 41:28–32). As a reward, Pharaoh put Joseph in charge of Egypt's grain supply.

> **"You meant to hurt me," [Joseph said.] "But God turned your evil into good."**
> **—GENESIS 50:20**

During the famine, Jacob sent the brothers to Egypt to buy grain (Genesis 42:1–3). When they met with Joseph, they didn't recognize him. In fact, they *bowed down to him*, fulfilling Joseph's childhood dream! When Joseph finally revealed his identity, his brothers were afraid. But filled with God's love, Joseph forgave them.

Joseph understood that God's love can turn even the worst situation into something beautiful and good.

What Are the Twelve Tribes of Israel?

Back in Bible days, it was common for men to have more than one wife. Jacob had four wives and was the father of twelve sons! Jacob's sons were Reuben, Simeon, Levi, Judah, Dan, Naphtali, Gad, Asher, Issachar, Zebulun, Joseph, and Benjamin—the ancestors of what became known as the twelve tribes of Israel. There was no tribe named Joseph, but two tribes were named after Joseph's sons, Manasseh and Ephraim. Each tribe had its own land. The tribe of Levi did not stay in one place but served all the tribes as priests.

The Twelve Tribes of Israel

Reuben
Simeon
Levi
Judah
Dan
Naphtali
Gad
Asher
Issachar
Zebulun
Joseph (Manasseh and Ephraim)
Benjamin

Like their forefathers, Jacob's sons and grandsons weren't perfect. Throughout their history, the twelve tribes struggled with God and with each other. Still, God chose them to be His people.

Eventually the tribes split up into two kingdoms: Judah in the south and Israel in the north. We know from the Bible that God's Son, Jesus, was a descendant of the tribe of Judah. John the Baptist was from the tribe of Levi. The apostle Paul was from the tribe of Benjamin.

Who Is Moses?

• • • • • • •

Moses is the most important prophet and heroic leader of the Jewish people. He is best known for leading the Israelites out of slavery in Egypt and to their promised land, and for delivering God's Ten Commandments. Moses is so important that he appears in the New Testament too, when he and the prophet Elijah meet up with God's Son, Jesus, at an event we call the transfiguration (Matthew 17:1–9).

> **There has never been another prophet like Moses. The Lord knew Moses face to face.**
>
> —DEUTERONOMY 34:10

Moses was an unlikely and reluctant leader. The Bible says, "Moses was very humble. He was the least proud person on earth" (Numbers 12:3)! When God called him to lead His people, Moses asked Him to send someone else! He was not a skilled speaker, and God eventually gave Moses permission to let his older brother, Aaron, speak for him (Exodus 4:14–16).

The important thing about Moses is that he loved and trusted his Father God with all his heart and soul and mind. And God loved him back. Despite his human weaknesses, when Moses was called by God, he obeyed. His faith in God was unshakeable, and God gave him everything he needed to be God's helper.

Who Is Joshua?

• • • • • • •

Joshua is known as one of the Bible's greatest military leaders and courageous men of faith. He was born a Hebrew slave in Egypt, and he went with Moses on their journey to the promised land. During the Israelites' forty years in the wilderness, Joshua was Moses' second-in-command.

The Bible says Moses changed Joshua's name from *Hoshea*, which means "salvation," to *Joshua*, which means "God is salvation" (Numbers 13:16). Scholars think Moses did this because of Joshua's extraordinary faith and closeness to God. Before Moses died, God told him to appoint Joshua to lead the Israelites into Canaan, the promised land (Numbers 27:18–21).

Entering Canaan would not be easy. There was the Jordan River to cross. There were giant warriors living there in great, fortified cities. Against all the odds, Joshua led the Israelites in many battles against fierce enemies. When God spoke, Joshua listened. It took Joshua seven years of fighting before the Israelites finally controlled Canaan, in fulfillment of God's promise.

Who Is Gideon?

• • • • • • •

Gideon was a famous warrior, leader, and prophet of the Jewish people. In the years after Joshua's death, God's children forgot about God and His laws. Because of their disobedience, the Israelites faced hard times. When enemies invaded, they cried out for help. Because God still loved His children, He heard their cries and answered.

Gideon was an ordinary person, but God saw his potential. God sent an angel to tell Gideon he'd been chosen to lead the Israelites. At first Gideon was not so sure about this. So he asked God to prove Himself by performing miracles! The first miracle took place when God's angel caused fire to shoot out of a rock (Judges 6:11–22). Because Gideon's faith was not so strong, he needed *more* signs. In the most famous story, Gideon told God: "I'm going to lay a piece of wool fleece on the ground. If You really want me to be Your leader, make the wool wet with dew in the morning and the ground dry." God did it!

You'd think that would satisfy Gideon. But no! The next night he asked for the opposite—dry fleece, wet ground. Again, God did it (Judges 6:36–40)! *Finally*, Gideon trusted God, stopped asking Him for signs, and led the Israelites to victory!

Who Is Ruth?

Ruth was from the ancient kingdom of Moab. The name *Ruth* means "friend." As you will see, this name describes Ruth perfectly!

The Moabites did not worship the God of Israel, but Ruth married an Israelite who did. Over time, Ruth came to know and love God. Sadly, Ruth's beloved husband, brother-in-law, *and* father-in-law died! Suddenly Ruth, her mother-in-law, and her sister-in-law were widows. Back then, widows had very hard lives—especially if they didn't have a family to provide for them.

But Ruth said, "Don't ask me to leave you! Don't beg me not to follow you! Every place you go, I will go. Every place you live, I will live. Your people will be my people. Your God will be my God."

—RUTH 1:16

The three widows were heartbroken. They had to decide what to do to survive. Ruth's sister-in-law decided to stay in Moab, where she had family. But her mother-in-law, Naomi, was moving back to her hometown of Bethlehem. Naomi tried to convince Ruth to stay in Moab, but Ruth could not bear it! She vowed to stay with Naomi always.

Ruth's faithful vow of loyalty and love is so famous that it's a passage that is often read aloud at weddings. Ruth went to Bethlehem with Naomi, and God blessed them both in surprising ways. To learn more about this loving friend, you can read Ruth's book in the Old Testament!

Who Is the Prophet Samuel?

A prophet is a person who speaks the true Word of God to people. Samuel was one of God's greatest prophets. The name *Samuel* means "God hears." Samuel's birth was God's miraculous answer to his mother Hannah's prayers for a son. When Samuel was about three years old, Hannah sent the boy to live with an old priest named Eli, who would be Samuel's teacher (1 Samuel 1). With all his heart and mind, Samuel wanted to hear God's voice. Then one night something amazing happened.

As Samuel was lying down to sleep, suddenly God called Samuel's name. But Samuel thought it was Eli calling! The boy ran to his teacher's bedside and said, "I am here. You called me." But Eli said no, he hadn't. Confused, Samuel went back to bed. Two more times this happened! Finally Eli realized the Lord was calling the boy. So he said, "If he calls you again, say, 'Speak, Lord. I am your servant, and I am listening'" (1 Samuel 3:2–10).

From then on, Samuel was filled with God's Holy Spirit and spoke freely with God. God told Samuel to *anoint*, or choose for service, the first and second Jewish kings—Saul and David.

Who Is the Prophet Elijah?

• • • • • • •

Elijah is among the most important of all God's prophets. The name *Elijah* means "my God is the Lord." Like Moses, Elijah was an ordinary, flawed human being who loved God. When Elijah's faith was strong, God used him to do amazing things. When Elijah's faith was weak, he lost confidence and got scared and depressed. Still, he never lost his faith or stopped listening to God.

Elijah's prophecies always came true—the sign of a true prophet. Filled with God's Holy Spirit, he also performed many miracles, including bringing a widow's dead son back to life (1 Kings 17:17–24)! Elijah is also famous for how he did not experience earthly death, but was miraculously swept up to heaven by God in a "whirlwind," riding a "chariot and horses of fire" (2 Kings 2:11)!

God promises that one day Elijah will return to earth to announce the coming of the Messiah (Malachi 4:5). Elijah is so important that he appears in the New Testament too, when he and Moses meet with Jesus in a supernatural event called the transfiguration (Matthew 17:1–3).

Who Is the Prophet Isaiah?

• • • • • • •

Isaiah (I-*zay*-ya) is one of the most famous and important of God's prophets. The name *Isaiah* means "God is salvation." In the New Testament, Isaiah is the most quoted book of the Old Testament, with 419 references! Isaiah served as a prophet for more than fifty years, from about 740 to 687 BC. He is famous for his amazingly detailed prophecies about God's promised *Messiah*, or anointed Savior of the world, which were fulfilled in Jesus (Isaiah 7:14). Isaiah's eager, willing, and obedient response to God's call is an inspiration for Christians everywhere. When God called for someone to do His work, Isaiah said, "Here I am. Send me!"

> **Then I heard the Lord's voice. He said, "Whom can I send? Who will go for us?"**
>
> **So I said, "Here I am. Send me!"**
>
> **—ISAIAH 6:8**

Today God continues to ask His children to be His helpers. When God calls your name, you—like Isaiah—can say, "Here I am! Send me!"

Who Is the Prophet Jeremiah?

• • • • • • •

Jeremiah is a major prophet, called by God when he was very young, about seventeen years old. The name *Jeremiah* means "God has lifted up." When God called Jeremiah, he responded, "I don't know how to speak. I am only a boy." But God said, "Don't say, 'I am only a boy.' . . . Don't be afraid of anyone, because I am with you" (Jeremiah 1:6–8). True to His word, God stayed with Jeremiah and told him exactly what to say.

Jeremiah lived during the dark, difficult days leading up to the downfall of Jerusalem. Sadly, the Jewish people didn't want to hear Jeremiah's dire prophecies. In fact, they turned their backs on him! This broke Jeremiah's heart, and he often wept for his fallen nation and people (Jeremiah 13:17). That's why he's known as "the weeping prophet."

Almost everyone abandoned Jeremiah, with one happy exception: a friend named Baruch, who helped Jeremiah write his book of prophecies, which you can read in your Bible today. How loving God is to provide good friends and helpers in times of need!

Who Are the Twelve Apostles?

• • • • • • • • •

The twelve apostles are the twelve men Jesus chose to be His *disciples*, or students, while He walked and talked on earth. The word *apostle* means "one who is sent out."

Simon Peter and his brother, Andrew, were fishermen on the Sea of Galilee. Jesus gave Simon the name *Peter*, which means "stone" or "rock" (Matthew 16:18).

Andrew was a fisherman who was very good at introducing people to Jesus—including his brother, Simon Peter.

James was also a fisherman. He was the older brother of John. James, Peter, and John were among Jesus' best friends.

John was the younger brother of James. Jesus' nickname for John and James was "Sons of Thunder" because they had very loud voices and big, bold personalities. John and Jesus were very close. Some scholars say that John was Jesus' best friend.

Philip was from the same town as Peter and Andrew (John 1:44). The name *Philip* means "lover of horses."

Bartholomew means "son of a farmer." Bartholomew was one of the eleven apostles who witnessed Jesus' ascension to heaven (Acts 1:1-13).

Thomas became known as "doubting Thomas" because he would not believe that Jesus had been raised from the dead until he could see Jesus' resurrected body with his own eyes. When Thomas reached out his hands and touched Jesus' wounds, he said, "My Lord and my God!" Then Jesus said to

Thomas, "Because you have seen me, you have believed; blessed are those who have not seen and yet have believed" (John 20:28–29 NIV).

Matthew was a tax collector. Because he collected money for the Romans, Matthew was considered a traitor by the Jews and nobody liked him. When Matthew met Jesus, he stopped being a tax collector and instead followed Jesus everywhere. He learned to love God and soon had many friends.

James was the son of Alphaeus. There were two apostles named James. He was also known as "James the Less," possibly because he was younger or smaller than James the brother of John.

Thaddaeus was more commonly known as Jude or "Judas son of James." John refers to Thaddaeus as "Judas," *not* to be confused with "Judas Iscariot" (John 14:22), who was another apostle.

Simon the Zealot had strong political views. To be *zealous* is to be "fervently passionate." In Jesus' day, the Zealots were a group of Jews who hoped for an earthly king to restore Israel to its former glory.

Judas means "praised one" but has also come to mean "betrayer" or "double-crosser." This is because Judas Iscariot is the disciple who betrayed Jesus, which led to His death on the cross (Matthew 26:14–16). Even though Judas did a terrible thing, God turned it into something beautiful and good for the whole world.

The twelve apostles were ordinary people, just like you and me. They were not highly educated, rich, or powerful. But through knowing and loving Jesus, they became extraordinary people. Filled with God's Holy Spirit, they traveled all over, risking their lives to share the story of Jesus with everyone they met. Preaching the good news about Jesus, they changed the world forever.

Who Is the Apostle Paul?

• • • • • • •

The apostle Paul's original name was *Saul*, which means "asked or prayed for." Saul was a brilliant, learned Jew who loved God but didn't understand how Jesus could be God's Son. In fact, he hated Christians so much that he persecuted them! The word *persecute* means "to chase in order to hurt someone."

When Saul heard about Christians in a town called Damascus, he could hardly wait to hunt them down and throw them in jail! On his way to Damascus, suddenly a bright light from heaven flashed around him. Saul heard a voice say, "Saul, Saul! Why are you doing things against me?" It was Jesus! Saul was so terrified that he fell to the ground. Jesus told Saul to get up and carry on his journey, and that He would tell him what to do next (Acts 9:3–6), which He did.

Saul was shocked by Jesus' total forgiveness and love for him. His heart was filled with God's Holy Spirit, and his life was totally turned around. He stopped persecuting Christians and shared the good news of Jesus' love with everyone he met. Because he was like a new man, Saul changed his name to the Greek name *Paul*, which means "small or humble." This also helped him more easily share the good news of Jesus with *Gentiles*, or people who aren't Jewish.

Who Is the Gospel Writer Matthew?

Matthew was a tax collector. The name *Matthew* means "gift of God." Because Matthew was a tax collector for the Romans, he was considered a traitor by his fellow Jews and had few friends. When Matthew met Jesus, he stopped being a tax collector. Jesus taught him how to love God and people more than money, and soon Matthew had many friends.

Matthew wrote his gospel around AD 60–70, or about thirty years after Jesus' ascension to heaven. Paying special attention to Jesus' teachings and sermons, Matthew wrote for a mostly Jewish audience. He wanted to prove to the Jews that Jesus was the long-awaited Messiah, or God's *anointed* ruler, descended from King David and Abraham. This is why Matthew opens his gospel with a long, detailed *genealogy*, or family history, of Jesus (Matthew 1:1–17). For us, this long list of names may not be so interesting, but for the Jewish people it was *very* important. It proved that Jesus was the long-prophesied "Son of David," King of the Jews.

Who Is the Gospel Writer Mark?

Mark's full name was John Mark. *John* means "God is gracious," and *Mark* means "warlike." Mark was a teenager when Jesus and His followers met in Mark's mother's house in Jerusalem. Scholars think Mark watched and listened to Jesus as He taught. He may have been present when Jesus died on the cross.

Mark wrote his gospel around AD 55–65. It is the earliest written and shortest gospel. It's full of action—Mark uses the word *immediately* around forty times!

Mark wrote his gospel for a largely *Gentile*, or non-Jewish, audience. He pointed out that Jesus described Himself as "the Son of Man" (Mark 8:31), who must suffer and die. The disciples didn't understand or like it when Jesus talked about Himself this way. But later they saw that Jesus was fulfilling the Old Testament prophecies about the Messiah dying for our sins (Isaiah 52:13–15, Isaiah 53). Jesus suffered and gave up His life for us so that our sins can be forgiven and we can live forever with God in heaven.

Who Is the Gospel Writer Luke?

Luke was a Greek-speaking doctor and dear friend of many in the early church. The name *Luke* means "light-giving." Luke is the only *Gentile*, or non-Jewish, author of the New Testament. Luke didn't know Jesus personally, but he carefully researched His life by speaking to many people who did. He was an excellent reporter.

Luke wrote his gospel around AD 60–70. Luke also wrote the book of Acts in the New Testament, which tells the story of the arrival of God's Holy Spirit on earth and the story of the early Christian church, including Paul's missionary travels. The gospel of Luke includes many details not found in the other gospels, paying special attention to Jesus' parables.

The gospel of Luke includes famous hymns, including the Song of Mary (Luke 1:46–55) and the *Gloria in Excelsis* sung by all the angels when Jesus was born. *Gloria in Excelsis* means "Glory to God in the highest!" The angels went on to sing, "And on earth peace, goodwill toward men!" (Luke 2:14 NKJV).

Who Is the Gospel Writer John?

John was one of Jesus' original twelve apostles. The name *John* means "God is gracious." Like his older brother, James, John was a fisherman from the Sea of Galilee. Jesus affectionate nickname for both John and James was "Sons of Thunder" (Mark 3:17). This is because John and James had very big voices and bold personalities!

Over time, John became especially close to Jesus. Many scholars believe that John was Jesus' best friend. John wrote his gospel around AD 70–90. He also wrote three letters in the New Testament and the book of Revelation.

The gospel of John is different from the other three gospels. John looks back in time at Matthew, Mark, and Luke, revealing their deep spiritual meaning. John does not begin his gospel with Jesus' birth. Instead, he goes back to *before* the creation of the world (John 1:1–14)! He does this to show how God, Jesus, and the Holy Spirit have always existed. He also shows us how God, Jesus, and the Holy Spirit relate to each other—and to each one of us—in an endless, eternal circle of life and love.

Who Is John the Baptist?

• • • • • • •

John the Baptist was Jesus' cousin. John's mother was Elizabeth, a cousin and good friend of Jesus' mother, Mary. Like Mary, Elizabeth loved and trusted God.

John was a prophet of God. A prophet is a person who speaks the true word of God to people. The word *prophet* means "one who speaks openly." John's mission in life was to tell people that Jesus truly was God's Son (John 1:15, 1:34).

John loved God with all his heart, mind, and soul. When John grew up, he told people to turn away from their sins. He told them to get ready for Jesus, who was coming soon. Some people thought John was crazy. But many others believed John and turned away from their sins. To show they had turned away from their sins, the people asked John to baptize or dip them in water. The water symbolized the washing away of their sins. Because John baptized people, he became known as "John the Baptist" (Matthew 3:1–12; Mark 1:1–8; Luke 3:1–20; John 1:6–8, 1:19–28).

Then Jesus came from Galilee to the Jordan to be baptized by John.
—MATTHEW 3:13 NIV

The most important person John baptized was Jesus. When John baptized Him, God's Holy Spirit came down from heaven like a dove. Then God's voice said out loud to Jesus, "You are my Son, whom I love; with you I am well pleased" (Matthew 3:13–17; Mark 1:9–11; Luke 3:21–22). This marked the beginning of Jesus' mission on earth. For the next three years, until His death on the cross, Jesus would preach and teach the message of God's love.

Who Is Lazarus?

• • • • • • •

Lazarus was a dear friend and follower of Jesus who lived with his two sisters, Mary and Martha. The name *Lazarus* means "my God has helped." When Lazarus died, Jesus was so heartbroken that He wept (John 11:35 NIV).

But then Jesus prayed to God, thanking Him (in advance!) for the miracle He was about to do. With a big shout—"Lazarus, come out!"—Jesus brought Lazarus back to life (John 11:43)! When Lazarus walked out of his tomb, everyone was *so* happy!

The story of Lazarus is true. But the resurrection of Lazarus is different from the resurrection of Jesus. Lazarus would die again, as all humans must. Jesus' resurrection body is one that never dies! Jesus is now in heaven in His resurrection body. Through God's Holy Spirit, He also lives in our hearts. One day Lazarus will receive his heavenly resurrection body—and so will all believers, including you!

THE OLD TESTAMENT

Why Does God's Name Sometimes Appear as "LORD" in the Old Testament?

• • • • • • •

God's name was so holy to the Jews that, out of reverence, they didn't write or say it out loud. They wanted to obey the third commandment.

The ancient Hebrew alphabet had no written vowels (*a*, *e*, *i*, *o*, or *u*). In the original Old Testament manuscripts, the name of God was written as four Hebrew consonants, which translate into English as YHWH or JHVH. This grouping of four letters is called the *Tetragrammaton*—which is a very big word!

> "You must not use the name of the Lord your God thoughtlessly."
> —EXODUS 20:7

Some English versions of the Bible add vowels to create the words *Yahweh* (*Ya*-way) and *Jehovah* (Je-*ho*-va). Most Bibles translate YHWH and JHVH as LORD (with big and small capital letters).

Even today some Jewish people will not write or say the name of God. Instead, they substitute the name *Adonai* (*Add*-on-eye), which means "my Lord," or *HaShem*, which means "the Name." Some Jewish people write the English word *God* with the middle letter deleted, so it looks like this: "G-d." All this is done out of reverence and a desire to obey God's law.

Was There Really a Worldwide Flood?

• • • • • • •

Yes, there really was a worldwide flood during the time of Noah! The name *Noah* means "comfort and rest." Noah was a faithful man who loved God. This was rare in his day, as humans had mostly forgotten God and grown evil. This broke God's heart (Genesis 6:5–6).

God warned Noah that a great flood was coming that would destroy all life. He gave Noah instructions for building a huge *ark*, or floatable container, that would save Noah and his family. God told Noah to take into the ark one pair of every living animal on earth! And then—just as God said—the rain fell and the earth flooded.

> **Water flooded the earth for 40 days. As the water rose, it lifted the boat off the ground.**
> —GENESIS 7:17

Everything was destroyed except the ark (Genesis 7:23). When the rain finally stopped, the ark came to rest in the mountains of Ararat, in modern-day Turkey. God filled the sky with a beautiful rainbow as a sign of His promise to never again destroy the earth by water (Genesis 9:12–15). Modern-day underwater archaeologists and geologists confirm that there truly *was* a huge flood in Noah's day. Scientific evidence shows it happened around 5000 BC.

Is It True That Moses Was Adopted?

• • • • • • •

When Moses was born, the twelve tribes of Israel had become slaves in Egypt. The Egyptian *Pharaoh* (*fare*-oh), or king, punished the Israelites by commanding that their male children be drowned in the Nile River!

For three months Moses' mother hid her newborn boy. When she could no longer hide him, she found a sturdy basket and waterproofed it with tar. With a heavy heart, she tucked her son in the basket and sent it floating among the reeds in the Nile. Of all people, guess who found him? Pharaoh's daughter! Upon seeing the sweet baby, her heart melted and she pulled the basket from the river. Best of all, she unknowingly hired Moses' mother to nurse and look after the child throughout his early years!

When Moses grew older, he was returned to Pharaoh's daughter, who officially adopted him. Pharaoh's daughter named the boy Moses, because she "had pulled him out of the water" (Exodus 2:10). The name *Moses* means "to draw out or deliver."

Then Moses lived in a palace. But Moses never forgot who he was and where he came from. He never stopped loving God and His people.

Is It True That God Spoke to Moses in a Burning Bush?

• • • • • • • •

Yes, it is true that God spoke to Moses through a burning bush. When God wants to get our attention, He can do anything! One day, Moses witnessed an Egyptian beating a Hebrew slave. Moses, a Hebrew himself, was so angry that he murdered the Egyptian! When Pharaoh found out, he sought to kill Moses. Fearing for his life, Moses fled to a faraway desert (Exodus 2:11–15). Moses was tending sheep when he noticed a strange sight. A bush was on fire, but not burning up.

Moses said, "I will go closer to this strange thing. How can a bush continue burning without burning up?"

—EXODUS 3:3

Then, Moses heard a voice calling him from the flames: "I am the God of your ancestors. I am the God of Abraham, the God of Isaac and the God of Jacob" (Exodus 3:6). *Holy smoke!*

God told Moses to lead the Israelites out of slavery in Egypt. "Who should I say sent me?" Moses asked. God replied, "Tell them, 'I AM sent me to you'" (Exodus 3:14). Because Moses loved and trusted God, he obeyed.

What Are the Ten Plagues of Egypt?

• • • • • • •

As God commanded, Moses returned to Egypt. There was a new Pharaoh when he arrived, and Moses and his brother, Aaron, met with him and asked him to set the Israelite slaves free. But Pharaoh refused. He ordered them to work even harder! The Egyptians believed in many false gods. It was up to Moses to show them the reality and power of the Israelites' one true God.

Plague comes from a Latin word that means "to strike or wound." The ten plagues of Egypt, listed here, were disasters allowed by God to change Pharaoh's mind (Exodus 7:20–12:30):

1. The Nile River turned to blood.
2. Frogs infested Egypt.
3. Gnats swarmed everywhere.
4. Flies swarmed everywhere.
5. All the livestock died.
6. Everyone suffered sores and boils.
7. A terrible storm destroyed the land.
8. Locusts ate their crops.
9. Darkness covered the land
10. Every Egyptian firstborn son died.

Through all of this, God miraculously protected the Israelites. Finally, overwhelmed by grief over the death of his firstborn son, Pharaoh agreed to let the Israelites go. At last he was convinced of the reality and power of the Israelites' one true God.

What Is Passover?

Passover is one of the most important Jewish holidays. It is an eight-day festival that takes place in the spring. Passover celebrates how God delivered the Israelites from slavery in Egypt.

We learned how God used ten plagues to convince Pharaoh to let His people go. The tenth and worst plague was the death of all firstborn males. God had saved the Israelites from the first nine plagues. But with the tenth plague, God required an act of faith on their part.

Through Moses, God commanded each Israelite family to take an *unblemished*, or healthy, male lamb and kill it. The blood of the lamb was to be smeared on the *lintels*, or top and sides of their doorways. The lamb was to be roasted and eaten that night.

God warned that at midnight, death would visit every house. The only protection for the Israelites was the blood of the sacrificed lamb. "The blood will be a sign. . . . When I see the blood, I will pass over you," God said (Exodus 12:13). This is how "Passover" got its English name. God kept His promise. He always does.

Is It True That Moses Parted the Red Sea?

• • • • • • •

Yes, it is true that with God's help, Moses parted the Red Sea. God can do anything!

After Pharaoh let the Israelites go, Moses led them to Egypt's border on the shore of the Red Sea. But suddenly Pharaoh changed his mind and ordered his great army to attack the Israelites. Oh no! Moses and his people were trapped between the advancing soldiers and the Red Sea. Here's what happened next.

Moses reached out his hand over the sea, and a great wind started blowing the waters back. Dry land appeared in the middle, between two walls of water. The Israelites moved forward, but the Egyptians followed. God slowed the Egyptians by confusing them and causing their chariots to break. As soon as the Israelites had crossed to the other shore, God told Moses to stretch out his hand again and bring the waters back down on the Egyptians. Moses obeyed, and all the soldiers were washed away!

When the Israelites saw this miracle with their own eyes, "they trusted the Lord and his servant Moses" (Exodus 14:31). This was important, because the Israelites had a long, hard journey ahead.

What Are the Ten Commandments?

• • • • • • •

God chose Moses to be His most important prophet and leader of the Jewish people. Moses loved and obeyed God. For generations, the Israelites had been without a home, held as slaves in Egypt. God chose Moses to lead them out of Egypt to Canaan, or "the promised land," which had been promised by God to Abraham's descendants (Genesis 12:7). In about 1300 BC, Moses led the Israelites out of slavery in what is called the *exodus*—a word meaning "a mass departure of people." Moses was a good leader, but still the people got into trouble. Like you and me, they were human. They needed rules to live by.

God loved His people. He wanted them to enjoy faith-filled, happy, healthy, meaningful lives. He called Moses to the top of Mount Sinai, where He wrote His rules for living on two stone tablets (Deuteronomy 10:1–5).

God's rules became known as the Ten Commandments. Even today the Ten Commandments form the basis for many of our laws and our ideas of right and wrong. They are all based on love—the unchanging love of God for all His children. And that includes *you*!

Here are the Ten Commandments from Exodus 20:1–17:

1. You must not have any other gods except me.
2. You must not worship or serve any idol. (An *idol* is any person, place, thing, or idea that's loved more than God.)
3. You must not use the name of the Lord your God thoughtlessly.

4. Remember to keep the Sabbath as a holy day. (The *Sabbath* is a day set aside for worship and quiet time with God.)
5. Honor your father and your mother.
6. You must not murder anyone.
7. You must not be guilty of adultery. (*Adultery* means "to be unfaithful to a marriage partner.")
8. You must not steal.
9. You must not tell lies.
10. You must not be envious.

The Ten Commandments are based on love.

What Is the Greatest Commandment?

• • • • • • •

In the New Testament, the Jewish religious leaders asked Jesus, "Which of the commands is most important?" Jesus answered . . . "Love the Lord your God. Love him with all your heart, all your soul, all your mind, and all your strength" (Mark 12:28–30). The leaders were testing Jesus. He answered correctly.

Hear, O Israel: The LORD our God, the LORD is one. Love the LORD your God with all your heart and with all your soul and with all your strength.
—DEUTERONOMY 6:4–5 NIV

This famous passage is part of the "Shema" prayer, which Jewish children learn from the earliest age. The Hebrew word *shema* means "Hear, O Israel" (Deuteronomy 6:4–5 NIV). Jesus' mother, Mary, and her husband, Joseph, would have recited the Shema with Him twice daily: once in the morning and again as a bedtime prayer. Mary and Joseph followed the command to teach their children about God's love and rules for living: "Talk about them when you sit at home and walk along the road. . . . Write them on your doors and gates" (Deuteronomy 6:7–9).

To this day, faithful Jews attach to their doorframes a small cylinder-shaped case containing a tiny parchment scroll with words from Deuteronomy. It's called a *mezuzah* (meh-*zoo*-zah), which comes from a Hebrew word meaning "doorpost."

What Is Manna?

• • • • • • •

After they left Egypt, and before reaching the promised land of Canaan, Moses and the Israelites spent forty years in the wilderness. Conditions were harsh, and they didn't have enough food.

God loved His children, so He miraculously provided Moses and the Israelites with a mysterious food called manna, which appeared each morning on the ground like a sweet, flaky dew or frost. The word *manna* is Hebrew for "What is it?," which was, of course, the question everyone was asking!

> **The Israelites called the food manna. It was white like coriander seed, and it tasted like honey wafers.**
>
> **—EXODUS 16:31 NLT**

Moses told the Israelites to quickly gather the manna each morning, before it melted in the sun. Each person was allowed a daily amount of one *omer*, or about 3.64 liters.

God provided manna for forty years. No one knows for sure what manna was made of, but the Bible says, "It was white like coriander seed, and it tasted like honey wafers" (Exodus 16:31 NLT). *Yum!* Sounds delicious! Once the Jews reached the promised land and began to farm food, the manna stopped appearing (Joshua 5:12).

Manna is a wonderful example of how our loving Father God meets His children's needs.

Is There Really a Lost Ark of the Covenant?

• • • • • • •

Yes, there really is a historic lost ark of the covenant! Remember the Ten Commandments? They were part of God's *covenant*, or agreement, with Moses and the Israelites. God wrote them for Moses on two stone tablets, and He gave detailed instructions for building an *ark*, or chest, to contain them. We call it the ark of the covenant (Exodus 25:10–22).

The ark was very beautiful and fancy, covered in pure gold. The lid was decorated with two golden *cherubim*, a kind of heavenly creature with wings (Exodus 25:17–22). During the Israelites' forty years in the wilderness, the ark of the covenant was housed in a special *tabernacle*, or tent for worshiping, in the desert. The ark of the covenant contained the holy presence and power of God!

The Jewish people carried it everywhere, especially into battles. Eventually it was placed in the first Jewish temple in Jerusalem. After the first temple was destroyed, the ark went missing. Today the whereabouts of the ark of the covenant is one of history's most fascinating unsolved mysteries.

What Are the Psalms?

• • • • • • •

The psalms are 150 beautiful poems and songs for worship. They were written over many centuries by different authors, including King David, King Solomon, and Moses. The Hebrew name for the book of Psalms was the book of Praises. That's because so many of the psalms are songs of praise to God. Although many of the psalms were written almost a thousand years before Jesus, some of them refer to Him! (Psalms 2, 16, 22, 23, 45, 110).

Many psalms were written by King David. God loved David, and King David loved God back. We know from the Bible that David loved to sing and dance. Many of his psalms are joyful. But because David was human, sometimes he made mistakes. Sometimes he was ashamed, brokenhearted, or afraid. So David also wrote psalms to tell God about his feelings.

The word *psalm* comes from the Greek word *psalmos*, which means "to pluck or play the harp."

Isn't it easy to imagine beautiful voices singing the psalms? We, like King David, can use psalms to sing to God about everything.

The book of Psalms is easy to find. It's right in the middle of your Bible!

What Is the Shepherd's Psalm?

• • • • • • •

The Twenty-third Psalm is the most famous of all the psalms. It is a beautiful song about God, written by King David of Israel. King David loved and trusted God with all his heart, just as a sheep trusts his shepherd. Because David actually worked as a shepherd when he was a boy, he knew what he was talking about. David recognized God's voice in his heart, just as a sheep recognizes his shepherd's voice. He depended on God to provide for his needs, just as a sheep depends on his shepherd to lead him to food, water, and safe shelter.

> **"I am the good shepherd. I know my sheep, and my sheep know me . . . I give my life for the sheep."**
> **—JOHN 10:14–15**

When you are worried or sad, the Twenty-third Psalm is a very comforting psalm to read. It also helps us understand what Jesus meant when He said, "I am the good shepherd" (John 10:11). The Twenty-third Psalm starts like this: "The Lord is my shepherd. I have everything I need. He gives me rest in green pastures. He leads me to calm water. He gives me new strength" (verses 1–3). Isn't that beautiful?

What Is a Proverb?

The book of Proverbs in the Old Testament was written mostly by Israel's good King Solomon, who was known for his great wisdom. Other contributors include a man named Agur, King Lemuel, and *anonymous*, or unnamed, scribes. A proverb is a pithy saying—easy to understand and remember—that offers practical advice for living a good life that pleases God. *Pithy* means "short, forceful, and to the point." The word *proverb* comes from the Latin *proverbium*, which means "to put forth a word." Proverbs are not promises. Rather, they are solid bits of hard-earned wisdom, based on commonsense truths.

To gain important wisdom, all you have to do is open your Bible to the book of Proverbs! Here are few famous ones to get you started:

- "The beginning of wisdom is this: Get wisdom." (Proverbs 4:7 NIV)
- "Trust the Lord with all your heart. Don't depend on your own understanding." (Proverbs 3:5)
- "A gentle answer will calm a person's anger. But an unkind answer will cause more anger." (Proverbs 15:1)
- "A happy heart is like good medicine." (Proverbs 17:22)

Does the Old Testament Say Anything About Jesus?

• • • • • • •

> **For to us a child is born, to us a son is given . . . And he will be called Wonderful Counselor, Mighty God, Everlasting Father, Prince of Peace.**
>
> —ISAIAH 9:6 NIV

God gave lots of exciting clues in the Old Testament about His Son, Jesus, coming to earth.

These clues are called *prophecies*. God gave these clues because He wanted His children to recognize Jesus when He arrived. God sent Jesus to earth to save His children—and that includes *you*! Finding prophecies about Jesus in the Old Testament is fun. It is like being a detective. Here are just some of the Old Testament prophecies about Jesus that are fulfilled in the New Testament:

- Jesus would be born of a virgin (Isaiah 7:14; fulfilled in Matthew 1:23–25).
- Jesus would be born in Bethlehem (Micah 5:2; fulfilled in Luke 2:4–7).
- Jesus would heal many (Isaiah 35:5–6; fulfilled in Matthew 8:16).

- Jesus is our "Good Shepherd" (Isaiah 40:11; fulfilled in John 10:11–14).
- Jesus would die with sinners (Isaiah 53:12; fulfilled in Matthew 27:38).

THE NEW TESTAMENT

What Are the Four Gospels?

• • • • • • •

The word *gospel* means good news (see the King James Version of Matthew 11:5; Luke 4:18, 7:22). The first four books of the New Testament are known as the four Gospels because they tell the good news about Jesus! The four Gospels are Matthew, Mark, Luke, and John. They were written by men who actually walked and talked with Jesus or knew people who did.

Matthew was a tax collector. Because he collected money for the Romans, nobody liked him. When he met Jesus, he stopped being a tax collector and followed Jesus everywhere. Matthew wrote his gospel around AD 60–70 (about thirty years after Jesus' death). The gospel of Matthew pays special attention to Jesus' teachings and sermons.

Mark was a teenager when Jesus and His followers met in Mark's mother's house in Jerusalem. Mark watched and listened to Jesus as He taught. Mark's full name was John Mark. He may have been present when Jesus died on the cross. Mark traveled with and learned a lot about Jesus from another disciple named Peter. He also traveled with the apostle Paul and Barnabas. Mark wrote his gospel around AD 55–65. It is the earliest written and shortest gospel. The gospel of Mark pays special attention to Jesus' miracles.

Luke was a Greek-speaking doctor. Luke didn't know Jesus personally, but he carefully researched His life by talking to many people who did know Jesus. Scholars agree Luke was a very good reporter! He traveled with Paul on some of his missionary trips.

Luke also wrote the book of Acts in the New Testament, which tells the story of the early Christian church. Luke wrote his gospel around AD 60–70. The gospel of Luke pays special attention to Jesus' parables.

John was a fisherman. When he met Jesus, John became one of the apostles and was the closest to Jesus. Some people think John was Jesus' best friend. John became a leader in the early church. In addition to his gospel, John also wrote three letters in the New Testament. It is believed that he also wrote the book of Revelation. John wrote his gospel around AD 70–90. The gospel of John pays special attention to how much God loves us.

Each of the four Gospels tells a slightly different story of Jesus because they come from four different people—Matthew, Mark, Luke, and John. This makes lots of sense. Imagine that four of your friends wrote a story about you. Parts would be the same. But because each friend knows you differently and you do different things together, parts would be different. All four stories together would give the best, most complete picture of you. Together, all four Gospels give the best, most complete picture of Jesus.

What Is the Golden Rule?

• • • • • • •

We learned how Jesus correctly answered the Jewish religious leaders' question about the greatest commandment. He went on to surprise everyone by adding this brand-new, equally important commandment: "Do to others what you would have them do to you" (Matthew 7:12 NIV).

Over the years, this has come to be known as the "golden rule." Why? Gold is of great value. The golden rule is of such great value that Jesus repeats it again in Luke 6:31. When we show God's love to others, we show God that we love Him.

> **"Love your neighbor as you love yourself."**
> —MATTHEW 22:39

Because we are human, following the golden rule is not always easy. What about days when we are down in the dumps? Or days when it's hard to love ourselves, much less others? Not to worry! The Bible promises that God's love has been poured into our hearts through the Holy Spirit (Romans 5:5). The Bible also promises that we are able to love because God first loved us (1 John 4:19).

When it comes to following the golden rule, God has given us all the love we need.

What Is a Parable?

A parable is a simple story that teaches a big idea. The word *parable* comes from a Latin word that means "comparison." When Jesus walked and talked on earth, He shared lots of important truths about God and His kingdom. Sometimes He did this by telling parables.

Jesus came to earth with an all-new message of God's love, and parables were an all-new way to share it.

For example, in the parable of the lost sheep, Jesus teaches how much God loves His children (Matthew 18:10–14). If one of His children wanders away like a lost sheep, God will leave the entire flock and search and search until He finds that child. For the common, everyday shepherd listening to Jesus, this would be a very impractical and extravagant thing to do! But that's how God's love is—surprising in every way. Remember that this parable is about how much God loves *you*—His very special child!

What Are the Epistles?

• • • • • • •

The epistles are a collection of letters in the New Testament. The word *epistle* (ee-*pis*-ell) means "to send a message." Another word for epistles is *letters*.

The New Testament letters were written by different men who lived at the same time as Jesus. Some of them actually walked and talked with Jesus! One of the most famous epistle writers was the apostle Paul.

The letters were written to teach and encourage early Christians in different communities in the ancient world. Some letters are named after the writer (James; Peter; John; Jude). Others are named after the people the letter was for (Timothy; Titus; Philemon; Hebrews). Still other letters are named after the places the letter was sent (Romans; Corinthians; Galatians; Ephesians; Philippians; Colossians; Thessalonians).

Today the epistles, or letters, of the New Testament still teach and encourage Christians around the world—including *you*!

What Are the Beatitudes and the Sermon on the Mount?

• • • • • • •

The word *beatitude* comes from a Latin word that means "happy." One day, after healing many people, Jesus climbed up a steep hill and began to teach. We call this the Sermon on the Mount (Matthew 5–7). In it, Jesus taught about what makes people truly happy.

> **Now when Jesus saw the crowds, he went up on a mountainside and sat down. His disciples came to him, and he began to teach them.**
>
> —MATTHEW 5:1–2 NIV

Over the years, nine of these famous teachings became known as the Beatitudes. I have a friend who calls them the "Be Attitudes," because they teach us how God wants us to be! You can find the Beatitudes in your Bible in Matthew 5:3–12. Remember when you read them that the word *blessed* means "happy." Here are the first five to get you started:

- "Blessed are the poor in spirit, for theirs is the kingdom of heaven."
- "Blessed are those who mourn, for they will be comforted."

- “Blessed are the meek, for they will inherit the earth.”
- “Blessed are those who hunger and thirst for righteousness, for they will be filled.”
- “Blessed are the merciful, for they will be shown mercy.”

Did Jesus Really Walk on Water?

• • • • • • •

Yes, Jesus really did walk on water.

> Peter said, "Lord, if that is really you, then tell me to come to you on the water."
>
> Jesus said, "Come."
>
> And Peter left the boat and walked on the water to Jesus. But when Peter saw the wind and the waves, he became afraid and began to sink. He shouted, "Lord, save me!"
>
> Then Jesus reached out his hand and caught Peter. Jesus said, "Your faith is small. Why did you doubt?" (Matthew 14:28–31).

Jesus did not walk on water to show off. He wanted to show Peter how important it is to keep your eyes on Jesus. When Peter took his eyes off Jesus, he lost his faith and sank. You might think that after seeing Jesus do so many awesome miracles, Peter and the disciples would have lots of faith. Sometimes they did. But sometimes they didn't. That's because Peter and the disciples were regular people, just like you and me.

PRAYER

What Is Prayer?

• • • • • • •

Prayer is a conversation with God. One part of a conversation is talking. The other part is listening. God created you to enjoy a personal relationship with Him. The more time you spend with God, the better you will get to know Him and the more you will grow to love Him.

God wants to listen to you (Psalm 34:15).

God is interested in all your thoughts and feelings. He's interested in all your friendships, hopes, and dreams. He's interested in everything about you (Psalm 139:1).

God wants to talk to you (Psalm 91:15).

God wants to comfort you when you are feeling sad, lonely, worried, or afraid. He wants to laugh with you when you are happy. He wants to help you when you have a difficult decision to make.

Why is God so interested in listening and talking to you?

Because God loves you (1 John 3:1).

It's as simple as that.

Do I Need to Use Special Words When I Pray?

• • • • • • •

You don't need to use special words when you pray. You don't need to use fancy language. You don't need to memorize prayers. You don't need to recite prayers written by other people. You don't need to write down your thoughts before you pray. You don't even need to speak out loud. It's perfectly fine to have a conversation with God silently. This is because God hears your thoughts (Matthew 6:8).

When you pray, just be yourself. Talk to God as if He is your best friend in the whole world. It is all right to cry when you pray. It is all right to laugh too.

Jesus was so close to God that when He prayed, He called God *Abba*, which in His native Aramaic language means "Daddy" or "Papa."

What should you pray about? Everything!

Can God Actually Talk to Me?

• • • • • • •

Yes, God can actually talk to you! The secret is to learn how to hear His voice. Sometimes that means taking time to be quiet and listen. This is not always easy to do. It is easy to be distracted by the TV. Or the sound of cars going by. Or the smell of chocolate-chip cookies. Sometimes it is easy to be distracted by the noise of your own thoughts!

God's voice is different from our thoughts. God often says things you might never think of yourself. Sometimes God speaks to you through a Bible verse or the words in a book or sermon. Many times God speaks through people we love.

Sometimes God speaks a tender word of comfort or a stern word of wisdom. He could give you a new spiritual idea or instruction. God always knows exactly what you need to hear (Isaiah 30:21). It's good to take time to listen to God!

Will God Answer My Prayers?

Yes, you can know for sure that God will answer your prayers. Jesus promised, "Whatever you ask for in prayer, believe that you have received it, and it will be yours" (Mark 11:24 NIV). Jesus also promised, "Ask and it will be given to you; seek and you will find; knock and the door will be opened to you" (Matthew 7:7 NIV).

God promises that He will answer your prayers.

Sometimes God's answers are not what we want to hear. Sometimes He answers "no" or "wait." God may not always give you what you want. But you can trust that God will always give you what you need. This is because God loves you and knows what's best for you. God always gives you the perfect answer to your prayer.

What Does It Mean to Pray in Jesus' Name?

Many Christians close their prayers with the words "in Jesus' name, amen." That's because Jesus said to the disciples, "If you ask for anything in my name, I will do it for you" (John 14:13). Saying the words "in Jesus' name" at the end of a prayer is not a magic formula. It doesn't guarantee that God will answer your prayer exactly the way you want. But it is a way of saying you know and love Jesus. You're saying, "Whatever You think is best for me, God."

You don't have to end every prayer with the words "in Jesus' name." This is because God doesn't care about the exact words you use when you pray. God does care that you mean what you say. When you pray, God wants you to speak to Him sincerely, from the bottom of your heart. Why is this? Because God loves you (1 John 3:1)!

Is It True That Jesus Is Praying for Me in Heaven?

• • • • • • •

Yes, it's true that Jesus is praying for you—right this very moment—in heaven!

After Jesus' resurrection, He ascended into heaven, where He is "at the right hand" of His Father (Romans 8:34 NIV), or at His right side. To be at God's right side means to be God's closest aide and helper.

> **Christ Jesus died, but that is not all. He was also raised from death. And now he is on God's right side and is begging God for us.**
>
> **—ROMANS 8:34**

One of the most important, loving things Jesus does as God's right-hand helper is intercede, or beg, for all of God's children in prayer. To *intercede* means "to earnestly ask on another's behalf." Because Jesus loves you, He's constantly speaking up for you. He's constantly reminding God of your choice to believe in Him, and in God too. Right now, even as you read these words, Jesus is singing your praises to God our Father. In fact, all of heaven is rejoicing that you believe in Jesus (Luke 15:10).

How loving Jesus is to intercede for all God's children—and that includes *you*!

Can God's Holy Spirit Help Me When I Pray?

• • • • • • •

Yes, it's true that God's Holy Spirit can help you when you pray!

Because we are human, we sometimes don't know what or how to pray. Maybe our problem is too complicated, or we don't really know all the facts. When this happens, we can trust God's Holy Spirit to do the praying!

God's Holy Spirit is alive in our hearts, eager to help us. When you feel confused about praying, start by inviting the Holy Spirit to help you. The apostle Paul put it this way: "The Spirit helps us in our weakness. We do not know what we ought to pray for, but the Spirit himself intercedes for us through wordless groans" (Romans 8:26 NIV). How wonderful that when we don't know what to pray, God's Holy Spirit powerfully intercedes for us, with words we could never think of ourselves. God thinks of everything! Why does God do this? Because He loves you.

What Is the Lord's Prayer?

• • • • • • •

When Jesus walked and talked on earth, the disciples noticed He had a different way of praying. Jesus didn't use fancy language or call attention to Himself when He talked to His Father God. When Jesus prayed, it was like He was talking to His best friend in the world.

One time Jesus was praying in a place. When he finished, one of his followers said to him, ". . . Lord, please teach us how to pray, too."
—LUKE 11:1

Jesus' disciples wanted to pray like He did. So they asked Him to teach them how. Jesus' answer became known as the Lord's Prayer. It's the most famous prayer in the world:

> Our Father which art in heaven, Hallowed be thy name. Thy kingdom come, Thy will be done in earth, as it is in heaven. Give us this day our daily bread. And forgive us our debts, as we forgive our debtors. And lead us not into temptation, but deliver us from evil: *For thine is the kingdom, and the power, and the glory, for ever.** Amen. (Matthew 6:9–13 KJV)

*This last line appears in the King James Version of the Bible, but because it does not appear in all translations, some Christian churches don't include it.

The opening line of the prayer might be so familiar that we don't think much about it. But there is a lot hidden in these six carefully chosen words. (In case you are wondering, *art* is simply an old-fashioned word for "is.") First, notice that Jesus didn't say "My Father." Jesus used the word *our* to remind us that we belong to the larger, worldwide family of God, which includes all Christians everywhere throughout history! The word *our* also reminds us that we are not alone. It reminds us of how God wants us to pray with and help each other through loving acts of kindness. Worshiping and working together are wonderful ways for Christians to be God's helpers on earth.

Then, "Our Father" reminds us of the awesome fact that we *share the same Father* in heaven as Jesus! In the Lord's Prayer, Jesus described our Father God's name as "hallowed." The word *hallow* means "holy, or set apart." Because God is holy, the Bible says that we are to honor, respect, and be in total awe of Him. Our holy God loves His earthly children perfectly (1 John 3:1)!

Jesus went on, "Thy kingdom come, Thy will be done in earth, as it is in heaven." (In case you are wondering, *thy* is simply an old-fashioned word for "your.") Jesus was talking about the kingdom of God, or heaven. Each time we share God's love with others, we help His kingdom "come," or break through on earth!

Then Jesus said, "Give us this day our daily bread." God loves us and wants us to be well-nourished in our bodies! We also need to feed our spirits. We can do this by praying, reading the Bible, and learning about God. In fact, you're feeding your spirit right now! *Yum!*

In the Lord's Prayer, Jesus said, "Forgive us our debts, as we forgive our debtors." The word *debt* means "something owed." A *debtor* is a person who owes a debt. A debt can be money, but it can also be something else, like a favor returned. Some Christian churches use the words, "Forgive us our *trespasses* as we forgive those who *trespass* against us." Here, the word *trespass* means sin. Jesus said, "If you forgive men their trespasses, your heavenly Father will also forgive you" (Matthew 6:14 NKJV).

The key word here is *forgive*, which means "to excuse or pardon." Jesus reminds us not only to ask for forgiveness but to forgive others too. This is because refusing to forgive causes deep anger, sadness, and spiritual sickness. There is an old saying that "being unforgiving is like drinking poison and expecting the other person to die." *Yikes!*

It is not always easy to forgive. But if we ask God to give us forgiving hearts, He will. Because God forgives us, we are able to forgive others.

At the end of the Lord's Prayer, Jesus prayed, "And lead us not into temptation." This is another way of saying, "God, lead me *away* from temptation!" We're all tempted to do things we shouldn't, but the good news is that God is always by our side, ready to grab our hand and pull us away from danger.

"For thine is the kingdom, and the power, and the glory, for ever. Amen."
—MATTHEW 6:13 KJV

Finally, He prayed, "Deliver us from evil." Evil, sin, and death entered the world when Adam and Eve gave in to temptation and disobeyed God. Now the world and all human beings are fallen and broken. This is not what God intended! The word *deliver* here means "to save or rescue." God loves us so much, He sent Jesus to rescue us from sin and death, so we can live forever with God and Jesus in heaven (John 3:16).

But for now, we live in a world where evil, sin, and death still exist. This is why it's not easy being human! Our heavenly Father understands how filled with danger life can be. Because He loves us, He wants to protect us and keep us safe!

The traditional ending to the Lord's Prayer comes from the King

James Version of the Bible, which was published in 1611. The word *thine* is simply an old-fashioned way of saying “yours.”

This beautiful conclusion to the world’s most famous prayer is a way of saying, “Everything belongs to You, our Creator and Father God! Your heavenly kingdom, and our planet earth, the sun and the moon and the stars . . . everything! How awesome You are! You alone are worthy of our praise and love. To You alone belong all the power and glory in heaven and on earth, forever and ever!”.

The final one-word line of the Lord’s Prayer, *Amen*, means “yes, it is certain” or “so be it.”

How loving Jesus is to teach this beautiful and powerful prayer to His disciples and all believers—including *you*!

What Is a Good Everyday Prayer?

• • • • • • •

One of my favorite prayers is the "Collect for Purity" from *The Book of Common Prayer*. *Collect* (*coll*-ect) is an old-fashioned word for a short prayer. Some churches say it before celebrating Communion. But like all prayers, it can be said anytime or anywhere! It goes like this:

> Almighty God, to You all hearts are open, all desires known, and from You no secrets are hid. Cleanse the thoughts of my heart by the inspiration of Your Holy Spirit, that I may perfectly love You, and worthily magnify Your holy Name. Through Christ Jesus our Lord, I pray. Amen.

The beautiful "Collect for Purity" is a wonderful, short everyday prayer. I like to say it when I water my garden! The sight and sound of the sparkling water raining down on the flowers reminds me of my Christian baptism and the power of faith in Jesus to wash away my sins. It reminds me of how God lovingly nurtures and grows my faith.

What Is a Good Bedtime Prayer?

Bedtime is a great time to talk to God. You can thank Him for the day you have just had. You can talk to Him about tomorrow. You can even ask God to send His angels to watch over you while you sleep (Psalm 91:11). You can use the quiet moments before you fall asleep as a time to listen for God's still, small voice.

Here's a popular bedtime prayer for children. The word *Thee* is an old-fashioned way of saying "You." The word *Thy* is an old-fashioned way of saying "Your."

> Now I lay me down to sleep. I pray Thee, Lord, my soul to keep. Let Thy love guide me through the night. And wake me with Thy morning light. God bless . . . (Here you can have fun listing everyone in the whole world you love and care about!). I pray all these things in Jesus' name. Amen.

What Should I Do When I Can't Think of What to Pray?

• • • • • • •

In the Bible, the book of Acts tells the story of the early church. Like Christians today, the first Christians prayed a lot! There is no certain way you *have* to pray, but when you need some guidance, think of the letters in the word *ACTS*.

A: *Adoration*, which means "to deeply love." Begin your prayer time by praising God. Tell God how wonderful He is, how much you love Him, and how much you appreciate His love too!

> **They all joined together constantly in prayer.**
> —ACTS 1:14 NIV

C: *Confession*, which means "to admit or acknowledge." Confess all the ways you've stumbled. Tell God you're sorry. Ask for His forgiveness.

T: *Thanksgiving*, which means "to thank" God for all the good things in your life. No matter what, there's always much to be thankful for.

S: *Supplication* is a big word that means "to humbly, earnestly ask." Tell God what's going on in your life. Share your prayer requests. Don't hold back. Remember: no request is too small or too big for God!

Is It Okay to Pray for Help on a Test?

• • • • • • •

Yes, it is okay to pray for help on a test. But prayer is not an excuse for not being prepared! Prayer is not a magic wand. God expects you to do your homework and study for tests. That's your responsibility.

On the day of the test, you might pray, "God, You know how hard I've studied for this test. Please help me not to be nervous. Help me remember everything I can and do my best. Thank You for caring so much. I love You! In Jesus' name I pray. Amen."

Give your worries to the Lord. He will take care of you. He will never let good people down.
—PSALM 55:22

If you have not done your homework or studied as you should, ask God to forgive you and help you be better prepared next time. If you are really struggling with your schoolwork, be sure to tell your mom and dad and teacher. They will want to work with you to help you do better.

God wants to help you do well in school too. God wants the best for you in all things (Jeremiah 29:11)!

Is It Okay to Pray for My Pet?

• • • • • • •

Yes, it is okay to pray for your pet! It is okay to pray for all of God's amazing animals.

Our pets are very special creatures. Our pets don't really belong to us; they are given to us on loan from God to love and care for. Loving and taking good care of our pets can help us understand how deeply God loves and wants to care for us.

Let me tell you about our little pug, Max. When we first got Max, he was just ten weeks old, a brand-new, fluffy, snuggly puppy. One day I was taking him for a walk when I bumped into my friend Gail. "*Oooh!*" she exclaimed. "What a cute little puppy!" She scooped Max up and held him close to her cheek—a warm, wriggly ball of snuffly pug kisses.

> **God made the wild animals, the tame animals and all the small crawling animals to produce more of their own kind. God saw that this was good.**
>
> —GENESIS 1:25

"Would it be all right if I prayed for him?" she asked.

"Okay," I agreed, although I had never heard of praying for a dog, or any kind of animal. But my friend's prayer changed our life with Max forever.

Gail scooped Max up into her arms and prayed, "Thank You, God, for bringing this precious little puppy into my friend Kitty's life. Help her provide Max with a safe, happy home. May he be a dog that only knows human kindness. In Jesus' name I pray. Amen."

May he only know human kindness, I thought. *What a beautiful prayer!* You can pray it too for your pet—or for any of God's amazing animals!

As years passed, I often remembered Gail's words—especially during challenges that came later in Max's life.

Human beings and animals are connected in a deep way, because we share the same Creator God. Pets especially trust and depend on their humans to care for them. Taking care of our pets is not always easy or convenient. It is a big responsibility! Even so, God trusts us to love and care for them. And we can always pray.

Why Do We Say "Amen" at the End of Prayers?

The word *amen* comes from the Hebrew language and means "Yes, it is certain" or "So be it."

We say "amen" at the end of a prayer to show that what we have said to God is true. We say it to show that we believe God has heard our prayer. We say it to show that we believe God will answer our prayer. God is real and loves us, and He always hears us when we pray.

It's as simple as that!

What Is the Most Important Prayer?

• • • • • • •

Maybe you know a lot about Jesus, but you're still not sure He is living in your heart. Not to worry! We all feel like that sometimes.

Do you hear Jesus knocking on the door of your heart? If you do, maybe it's time to open the door. It's easy. Just say:

> Thank You, Jesus, for being real and loving me so much that You died on the cross for me and my sins. Thank You, Jesus, for forgiving me when I sin and loving me no matter what. Please come into my heart now, live in me, and be my friend forever. Day by day, show me how to live. In Your name I pray, Amen.

"Here I am! I stand at the door and knock. If anyone hears my voice and opens the door, I will come in."
—REVELATION 3:20

Guess what? You just prayed the most important prayer in the world! You may not *feel* any different, but you *are*. Jesus is living in your heart, which means you're about to go on a big adventure! Tell your mom or dad or other trusted grown-up who loves Jesus. They will want to celebrate with you and help you start your journey of faith!

CHRISTIANITY

What Is Religion?

• • • • • • •

Religion comes from the desire God has put in every human heart to try to get closer to Him. Religion is commonly defined as a "set of beliefs" about being human.

The word *religion* is rooted in the Latin word *ligare*, which means "bound together." When you add the letters *re* in front of *ligare*, you get *re-ligare*, or religion. So it means "to *re*-bind or *re*-connect together" something that has come undone. Hiding in this little word is the very big idea that God wants us to *reconnect* with Him!

The Bible teaches us that God created us to be in a loving, personal, two-way relationship with Him. Because God loves us, He wants us to know Him and love Him back.

Of all the religions in the world, Christianity is the only one that offers believers a completely and perfectly restored relationship with God through faith in His Son, Jesus (John 3:16). This is very good news!

What Is Christianity?

• • • • • • •

Christianity is a religion based on the life and teachings of Jesus Christ. Christianity began with a few disciples more than two thousand years ago. People who believe in and follow Jesus Christ are called Christians. The early believers were originally called followers of "the Way" because they followed the way of Jesus (Acts 9:2 NIV). They were first called "Christians" in the city of Antioch, which is located in modern-day Turkey (Acts 11:26).

The Bible records that the early Christians "devoted themselves to the apostles' teaching and . . . to prayer. . . . And the Lord added to their number daily those who were being saved" (Acts 2:42, 2:47 NIV). From Jerusalem, Christianity quickly spread to other places.

Today Christians live in every nation of the world. More than two billion people, or about one-third of the people on earth, call themselves Christians. It's estimated that more than 700 million Christians are fifteen years old or younger. That's a lot of Christian kids!

What Is the Difference Between Christianity and Other Religions?

• • • • • • •

Christianity is not just another religion that teaches *about* God. It's about having a *personal relationship with* God through faith in His Son, Jesus. God is alive and has a special plan for each person. Christians do not worship teachings and rules, but a living, loving God!

Christianity is different because the Bible says that God knows and loves His children even before they are born (Psalm 139:13–16)! God's deepest desire is for His children to know and love Him too (1 John 3:1).

Christianity is also different from many other religions because Christians believe our human bodies are very important. The Bible teaches that all of God's creation—including our bodies—is beautiful and good, and God uses our bodies to accomplish His will on earth (1 Corinthians 6:19–20). Christianity is not just a set of "pie in the sky" beliefs. It's a very real, practical faith, rooted in love, that God uses to offer hope in a broken world. How exciting it is to be a Christian!

Christianity is about having a *personal relationship* with God through faith in His Son, Jesus.

What Is Faith?

• • • • • • •

The Bible teaches, "Faith means being sure of the things we hope for. And faith means knowing that something is real even if we do not see it" (Hebrews 11:1). The word *faith* means "to trust and believe with confidence."

Faith is a gift from God, your Creator and heavenly Father. Here is good news: when you are born as God's child, you come hardwired with faith! Faith is not something that you have to scrunch up your eyes and nose and try to muster up. It's as natural as breathing. It is already planted in your heart. Jesus says that all it takes is faith no bigger than a *teeny-tiny mustard seed* to do great and beautiful things for God!

> **"Truly I tell you, if you have faith as small as a mustard seed . . . Nothing will be impossible for you."**
> —MATTHEW 17:20 NIV

Would you like your faith in God to grow? Then here's more good news: all you have to do is ask God to grow your faith, and He promises that He will! Why does God want to help your faith grow? Because God loves you (1 John 3:1).

Would you like more faith? Ask God, and He will give it to you.

What Is the Apostles' Creed?

• • • • • • •

The Apostles' Creed dates from the very early days of the Christian church. The word *creed* means "I believe." Knowing what you believe is important.

Belief in God is a very good and powerful thing. Jesus said, "All things are possible for him who believes" (Mark 9:23).

The Apostles' Creed is the most popular summary of Christian beliefs. Saying the Apostles' Creed helps Christians remember what they believe. To this day, the Apostles' Creed is said by Christians in churches around the world.

> I believe in God, the Father Almighty, creator of heaven and earth. I believe in Jesus Christ, his only Son, our Lord. He was conceived by the power of the Holy Spirit and born of the Virgin Mary. He suffered under Pontius Pilate, was crucified, died, and was buried. He descended to the dead.* On the third day he rose again. He ascended into heaven, and is seated at the right hand of the Father. He will come again to judge the living and the dead. I believe in the Holy Spirit, the holy catholic church**, the communion of saints, the forgiveness of sins, the resurrection of the body, and the life everlasting. Amen.

*Some churches do not include this line.
** *Catholic* means "universal" and does not refer to the Catholic denomination.

What Is Sin?

God is perfect. Human beings are not.

Sin is the imperfect condition of the human body, mind, and soul. The word *sin* comes from an Old English word that means "guilty." Sin is part of our human nature. It's the way we are born. Human beings make mistakes. We forget how to love. Sometimes we're selfish or unkind. Sometimes we do bad things on purpose. Sin is what separates us from God. It's why we need Jesus to be our Savior.

Sins are unloving thoughts, words, and behaviors. When a person thinks, *Oh, she is so stupid* or *He's such a jerk*, those are sinful thoughts. When a person cheats on a test, or gossips about a friend, or tells a lie, or steals a candy bar, those are sinful behaviors.

Everyone is born with a sinful human nature (Romans 3:23). It's all part of being human.

There was only one person ever born without a sinful nature. That person is Jesus (Hebrews 4:15).

THE CHURCH

What Is the Church?

• • • • • • •

The worldwide church is made up of all the Christians on earth. The early church was made up of people who lived mostly in the Middle East, northern Africa, and southern Europe. Today Christians live in every nation of the world!

The word *church* comes from an Old English word that means "Lord's house." That word suggests a building. The original New Testament Greek word for "church" is *ecclesia*, which means "assembly" or "congregation." This makes sense, because the church is more about people than buildings. The Bible describes the church as the living body of Jesus at work in the world! The church is a living example of God's love for the world and all the people in it.

The church is Christ's body. The church is filled with Christ, and Christ fills everything in every way.

—EPHESIANS 1:23

Because Christians have God's Holy Spirit living in their hearts, they can be God's helpers on earth. As the living body of Jesus, Christians help God's kingdom break through and touch others with His reality and love (Luke 4:43, 10:9).

What Is Baptism?

• • • • • • •

In Jesus' day, people who wanted to turn away from their sins and toward God were baptized. They waded into a river where John the Baptist dipped them in the water and said a prayer. The word *baptize* means "to dip." Water symbolizes the "washing away" and forgiveness of sins.

Baptism was very important to Jesus. Jesus was baptized when He was thirty years old, right when He started His ministry (Matthew 3:13–17 NIV). He had no sins that needed to be "washed away," but He was baptized out of loving obedience to His Father God and to set an example for us. Later, before ascending to heaven, Jesus told His disciples, "Go and make followers of all people in the world. Baptize them in the name of the Father and the Son and the Holy Spirit" (Matthew 28:19). The disciples loved Jesus and obeyed.

From the very earliest days of the church, believers in Jesus were baptized.

Over the ages, Christian churches around the world have developed different ways of doing baptisms. Some baptize babies and young children. Other churches require that children be old enough to make their own decision to be baptized. Sometimes adults are baptized. You are never too old to be baptized! Some churches sprinkle or pour water over the head of the person being baptized. Other

"Change your hearts and lives and be baptized, each one of you, in the name of Jesus Christ for the forgiveness of your sins."

—ACTS 2:38

churches have special indoor pools deep enough for a grown-up to be dipped totally underwater. Christians around the world are also baptized in rivers, ponds, oceans, and swimming pools.

Sometimes baptism is called "holy baptism." The word *holy* means "set apart by and for God." A baptism is a time of great rejoicing and celebration and is often followed by a special meal or party for family and friends!

Why is baptism so important to Christians around the world? Because Jesus asks us to do it (Matthew 28:19).

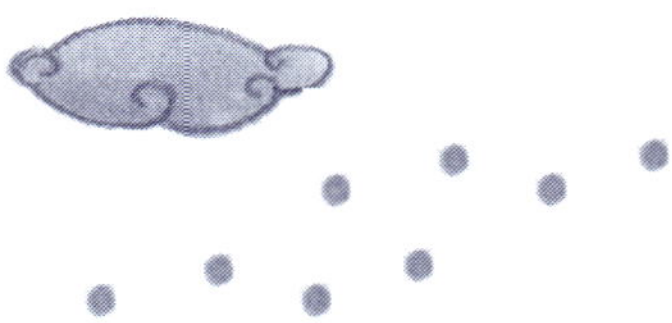

What Is a Godparent?

• • • • • • •

What do you think when you hear the word *godparent*? I always used to think of the fairy godmother in *Sleeping Beauty*! That changed when my best friend asked *me* to be her son Joshua's godmother. What an honor! But what did being a godparent mean?

My pastor explained that godparenting goes back to the early Christian church, when believers were persecuted and people lived shorter lives. A godparent is a *steward*, or guardian of faith, for a newly baptized child, helping make sure the child is raised knowing God and Jesus, and is involved in the church. A godparent can pray; give fun, faith-building gifts; and remember the anniversary of the godchild's baptism.

As soon as I learned what being a godparent meant, I called my friend back and said, "*Yes, yes, yes*, I would *love* to be Joshua's godmother!" I'm going to say a prayer for him right now. While I'm at it, I'll say a prayer for you too!

What Is Communion?

• • • • • • •

On the night before His death, Jesus shared a special Passover meal with His disciples. This meal is now known as the Last Supper.

The apostle Paul wrote:

> The Lord Jesus, on the night he was betrayed, took bread, and when he had given thanks, he broke it and said, "This is my body, which is for you; do this in remembrance of me." In the same way, after supper he took the cup, saying, "This cup is the new covenant in my blood; do this, whenever you drink it, in remembrance of me." (1 Corinthians 11:23–25 NIV)

From the very earliest days of the church, believers gathered to break bread and pray together (Acts 2:42, 20:7). To "break bread" means to eat and drink, or share a meal with others, or to enjoy each other's company. When the early Christians did this, they remembered Jesus and felt His presence and love in a powerful way.

This gathering together to share the "body and blood" of Jesus became known as "Communion." The word *communion* means "to participate together."

Churches *celebrate* or offer Communion in many different ways.

Some churches celebrate Communion at every service. Others do it once a month or twice a year. Some churches use wine. Others use grape juice. Some churches use bread. Some churches use flat crackers or thin wafers. Different churches have different names for Communion. Some call it holy Communion, the Great Thanksgiving, or holy Eucharist. The word *Eucharist* comes from a Greek word that means "thanksgiving." Other churches call it the

> **"Take this bread and eat it. This bread is my body."**
> —MATTHEW 26:26

Lord's Supper, the mass, the divine liturgy, or the breaking of bread.

When Christians celebrate Communion, the wine or grape juice represents Jesus' blood, which He shed for our sins when He suffered on the cross. The bread represents Jesus' body, which He gave up for our sins when He died on the cross. That's why some churches call the Communion bread the *host*, which means "the sacrificed one." Communion helps us experience the presence and love of Jesus in our hearts and bodies in a deeply real and powerful way.

Why is Communion so important to Christians? Because Jesus asks us to do it (Luke 22:18–20).

What Does It Mean to Be Born Again?

• • • • • • •

To be *born again* is another way of saying "to be converted from unbelief to belief in Jesus." The phrase comes from a famous conversation Jesus had with a Jewish religious leader named Nicodemus. One night Nicodemus came to Jesus and said, "We know that you are a teacher sent from God. No one can do the miracles you do, unless God is with him."

Jesus replied, "I tell you the truth. Unless you are born again, you cannot be in God's kingdom."

"But if a man is already old, how can he be born again?" Nicodemus asked. "He cannot enter his mother's body again."

Jesus answered, "I tell you the truth. Unless you are born from water and the Spirit, you cannot enter God's kingdom" (John 3:2–6).

When you convert from unbelief to belief in Jesus, you receive a brand-new life. This is because the moment you choose to believe in Jesus, God's Holy Spirit comes to live in your heart and you are spiritually born again. Isn't that amazing?

Why Do We Sing in Church?

• • • • • • •

Singing is a way to praise God. There is an old saying: "He who sings prays twice!" That's because when we sing, we praise God with words and song.

Singing is an important part of worship in almost all Christian churches. Thousands of years ago, King David and King Solomon wrote and sang songs of praise to God, which can be found in the book of Psalms in your Bible. Jesus and the disciples sang songs together too (Matthew 26:30). Singing makes your heart glad. God often speaks to His children through music and the words of hymns. What's your favorite spiritual song?

Sing psalms, hymns, and spiritual songs with thankfulness in your hearts to God.

—COLOSSIANS 3:16

"Jesus Loves Me" is one of the world's best-loved songs for kids. Maybe you know the tune. If so, feel free to sing the words!

Jesus loves me! This I know, for the Bible tells me so;
Little ones to Him belong, they are weak, but He is strong.
Yes, Jesus loves me! Yes, Jesus loves me!
Yes, Jesus loves me! The Bible tells me so.

How fun it is to sing songs of praise to God!

What Is a Doxology?

• • • • • • •

A doxology is an expression of praise to God, typically sung as a short hymn, or song of praise, in a church service. The word *doxology* comes from a Greek word that means "a saying of glory." Although the word *doxology* doesn't appear in the Bible, people of faith have been saying and singing God's praises for thousands of years. God is so wonderful, there are countless reasons to praise Him—including His love, His blessings, and His total awesomeness! In 1674, an English pastor named Thomas Ken wrote a beautiful doxology that touches on all three of these qualities of God. The doxology called "Praise God from Whom All Blessings Flow" is sung in many churches today. If you know the tune, why not sing it out loud? God loves it when His children sing His praises!

Praise God, from whom all blessings flow;
Praise Him, all creatures here below;
Praise Him above, ye heavenly host;
Praise Father, Son, and Holy Ghost! Amen.

How wonderful it is to praise our great and glorious God, from whom all blessings flow!

What Is a Missionary?

• • • • • • •

Jesus commanded His followers, "Go into all the world and preach the Good News to everyone" (Mark 16:15 NLT). Over the years, this powerful command has become known as the Great Commission. The word *commission* means "authority that is given to someone." Jesus' last words on earth granted authority to the disciples to go out and tell the whole world about God's love.

A Christian missionary is a person who shares the love of Jesus with others. The word *missionary* means "one who is sent off." Some missionaries travel to far parts of the world to share the love of Jesus. Other missionaries work close to home. Some missionaries work deep in the jungle. Other missionaries work in the world's biggest cities. Some missionaries teach villagers how to plant crops and dig wells for fresh water. Other missionaries build schools and hospitals. Some missionaries work with adults. Other missionaries work with teenagers and children.

Everyone who loves Jesus is a missionary. This is because wherever you are, you can share the love of Jesus with others. You can share the love of Jesus at home with your family. You can share the love of Jesus with your relatives. You can share the love of Jesus with your friends at school.

You are a missionary!

Why Do Some Crosses Have Jesus on Them and Others Don't?

• • • • • • •

Around the world and over the ages, the cross has become a symbol for Christianity. That's because through Jesus' obedient, sacrificial death on a cross, God offers salvation to the world and all the people in it! In Jesus' day, death on a cross was a shameful and painful death for criminals. Now it stands for Jesus' love!

In many Christian churches, the cross is displayed for all to see. Some crosses are simple and plain. They may be made of carved wood or metal.

Crosses that are empty symbolize the *risen* Jesus, who is now in heaven sitting at the right hand of His Father.

Other crosses include an image of Jesus during His time of loving sacrifice and suffering. A cross with the figure of Jesus is known as a crucifix. The word *crucifix* comes from a Latin word that means "fixed to a cross."

No longer is the cross a symbol of shame. It's a beautiful symbol of God's great love for the world and for all His children—including *you*!

What Is an Altar Call?

• • • • • • •

Some Christian church services end with an "altar call." The word *altar* refers to the front of the church. At the altar call, the pastor invites people who sense God calling them to give their lives to Jesus to walk to the front of the church. There they are tenderly greeted by the pastor and laypeople, who welcome and pray with them.

Some churches sing hymns during altar calls, such as "Softly and Tenderly Jesus Is Calling," part of which appears here. Remember: You don't have to be in church to commit your life to Jesus. You can respond to Jesus anytime, anywhere. You can respond to Jesus right now!

> *Softly and tenderly Jesus is calling, calling for you and for me;*
> *See, on the portals* He's waiting and watching, watching for you and for me.*
> *Come home, come home, you who are weary, come home;*
> *Earnestly, tenderly, Jesus is calling, calling, "O sinner, come home!"*

*Just in case you are wondering, the word *portal* means "a gateway or entrance" and refers here to the gates of God's kingdom.

What Is a Denomination?

• • • • • • •

The word *denomination* comes from a Latin word meaning "to give a name to." Today there are many different kinds of churches that make up the great, big Christian family of believers working together, each in their own way, to share God's love around the world. If we think of the worldwide Christian church as God's living tree, the many denominations are like the leaves of the tree. The major branches of the tree remain strong, but some leaves last only for a season.

It's a good idea for Christians to not spend too much time focusing on our differences. Instead, God wants us to love and pray for each other. He wants us to focus on and rejoice in the important things we share. When believers in the early church disagreed about this or that, here is what the apostle Paul wrote: "There is one Lord, one faith, and one baptism. There is one God and Father of everything" (Ephesians 4:5–6). In other words, when it comes to loving and serving Jesus, we're all on the same team!

Is It Okay for Me to Invite a Friend to Visit My Church?

• • • • • • •

Oh, what a delightful question! To invite a friend to church is a very loving and generous thing to do. When you invite a friend to church, you are sharing your love for Jesus. This makes God very happy!

God's church is like a beautiful lamp shining in the darkness. Jesus said, "No one lights a lamp and then covers it with a bowl or hides it under a bed. Instead, he puts the lamp on a lampstand so that those who come in will have enough light to see" (Luke 8:16). When we invite others to church, we are sharing the light of God's love. At church, we share the good news of God's love through Jesus (John 3:16). At church, we worship God. It's where Christians pray, learn about the Bible, make new friends, and put God's love into action. For all these reasons, church is a wonderful place for a friend to visit. Before you invite a friend to church, be sure to ask your mom and dad.

When you invite a friend to church, you are sharing your love for Jesus.

What Should I Do When I Think a Church Service Is Boring?

• • • • • • •

Everyone gets a little sleepy or bored during a church service sometimes. It's not always easy to sit still indoors when outside the sun is shining. It's not always easy to stay awake if you stayed up late the night before. It's not always easy to pay attention if the preacher is talking about something that is difficult to understand.

Here are a few ideas to help you the next time you find yourself a little bit sleepy or bored:

Tell God how you feel, and ask Him to help you.
Make a list of all the things you are thankful for.
Make a list of nice things you might do for other people.
Read the Bible. (Genesis, the first book in the Bible, is a good place to start.)
Pray for all the people you love.
Close your eyes and see if you can hear God whisper to you in your heart (1 Kings 19:12).

When you ask Him, God will lead your thoughts to Him!

CHRISTIAN SEASONS, HOLIDAYS, AND TRADITIONS

What Is Lent?

Lent is a season of forty days, not counting Sundays, before Easter Sunday. The word *Lent* comes from the Old English words *lencten*, which means "spring," and *lenctentid*, which means "springtide," and it was also the word for the month of March. Because the date for Easter changes from year to year, the start of Lent changes from year to year too.

Jesus ate nothing for 40 days and nights. After this, he was very hungry.
—MATTHEW 4:2

Before Jesus began to teach, He spent forty days in the desert. There, Jesus fasted and prayed. To *fast* means "to not eat any food." Fasting and praying helped Jesus grow very close to His Father God. When Satan came to tempt Him, He did not give in to sin!

During Lent, many Christians spend extra time with God. They pray and read the Bible. Sometimes they give something up to help others. For example, they give the money they would otherwise spend on candy or video games to help people in need.

Lent is a time to grow closer to God through prayer and to share God's love with others.

What Is Holy Week?

Holy Week is the final week of Lent and the week before Easter. It's a time when Christians around the world remember the week leading up to Jesus' death and resurrection.

The two best-known days of Holy Week are Palm Sunday and Good Friday. Palm Sunday is the first day of Holy Week. Good Friday is the Friday before Easter Sunday. Holy Week is a time to think and pray about God's great love for us and prepare our hearts for Easter.

Of all the Christian holidays, Easter is the most important. Why? Because the story of Easter shows us the incredible goodness and love of God. Through Jesus' life, we see God's desire to forgive and heal us. Through Jesus' death on the cross, we see God's deep desire to save us from our sins. Through Jesus' resurrection, we see how much God loves life—so much that He wants us to live with Him forever in heaven!

What Is Palm Sunday?

• • • • • • •

Palm Sunday is the first day of Holy Week, leading up to Easter Sunday. It's a time when Christians remember when Jesus rode into Jerusalem on a young donkey.

The week before His death, Jesus traveled to Jerusalem to celebrate the Passover meal with His disciples. Crowds of people threw their *cloaks*, or capes, on the road. They waved palm branches in the air to celebrate. "Hosanna!" they cried. "Blessed is he who comes in the name of the Lord!" (Matthew 21:1–11 NIV). The word *hosanna* or *hosannah* means "save us, I pray."

The people in the crowd loved Jesus. They had no idea that in less than a week, He would die on the cross—and that three days later, He would rise from the dead. But they were happy to welcome Him.

On Palm Sunday, some churches today pass out freshly cut palm branches. They might wave them in the aisles or weave them into the shape of a cross. The palm branches remind us of when Jesus rode into Jerusalem on a donkey.

What Is Good Friday?

• • • • • • •

Good Friday is the Friday before Easter. It is the day during Holy Week when Christians remember the day Jesus died (Luke 23:26–56). Many churches hold special services to remember the time when Jesus suffered on the cross.

The Good Friday church service is very somber and quiet. It is a time to pray and to remember that God loves us so much that He was willing to give up His only Son, Jesus, to die for us (John 3:16). We also remember that Jesus loves us so much that He was willing to die for us (John 15:9). There is no greater love than this (John 15:13).

At first glance, Good Friday might not seem "good" at all. Jesus suffered terribly and died. But because of Good Friday, there is much good news.

Because of Good Friday, we can thank God for Easter—for Jesus' resurrection and for forgiving our sins. We can thank God that we will join Jesus and live forever with Him and God in heaven!

On Good Friday, we remember that nothing, not even death, can separate us from God's love (Romans 8:38–39).

Why Is Easter So Important?

• • • • • • • •

Easter is the most important Christian holy day of the year. It is also the most important day in human history. On Easter Sunday, Christians around the world gather to remember and celebrate the fact that Jesus rose from the dead, completing God's mission for Him to save the world and all the people in it (Mark 16:1–8).

They celebrate with joyful prayers and singing. In the United States, many churches have special sunrise services and meet in the early morning darkness. On hillsides and beaches, they wait for the Easter morning sunrise. As the day dawns, they celebrate the fact that Jesus is not dead, but truly alive! The rising sun symbolizes the light of God's risen Son, Jesus.

> "The Lord really has risen from death!"
> —LUKE 24:34

Because Jesus rose from the dead, the dark power of evil, sin, and death is forever broken. How surprised and happy everyone was to see Jesus alive! Not even Jesus' family and closest friends ever expected such a miracle. Because Jesus is alive and we believe in Him, we can live forever with Him and God in heaven too. This is very good news!

Why Do We Light Candles on Easter?

• • • • • • •

Candlelight is a symbol of Jesus' victory over the darkness of evil, sin, and death. Lighting candles in church reminds us of Jesus' love, which lives and shines in our hearts.

Jesus described Himself as "the light of the world." Jesus told His disciples that they are "the light of the world" too (Matthew 5:14 NIV)! He went on to explain, "Let your light shine before others, that they may see your good deeds and glorify your Father in heaven" (Matthew 5:16 NIV). We can do the same!

> **"I am the light of the world. The person who follows me will never live in darkness. He will have the light that gives life."**
>
> **—JOHN 8:12**

The day before Easter is known as Holy Saturday or Easter Eve. Many churches celebrate it with a nighttime vigil service. A *vigil* is a special time for prayer. On Easter Eve, some churches turn out all the lights until the stroke of midnight, when the leader lights a tall white *paschal*, or Easter, candle. Everyone else lights their smaller candles from it, until the church is filled with light, and it's Easter morning! The light-filled church is a symbol of the risen Jesus, the "light of the world."

What Is Pentecost?

Pentecost is the name of an ancient Jewish festival that takes place about fifty days after Passover. The word *Pentecost* means "fiftieth day."

At the first Pentecost, about ten days after Jesus ascended into heaven, the disciples gathered in Jerusalem. Like the sound of a rushing wind, God's Holy Spirit arrived and filled their hearts with His love, truth, and power. They spoke about God's love in languages they did not know. Their lives were changed forever. Many new people came to believe in Jesus. It was truly a miracle (Acts 2)! It was also the beginning of the Christian church.

For Christians, Pentecost is celebrated on the seventh Sunday (about fifty days) after Easter. It is a time when Christians celebrate the arrival of the Holy Spirit on earth. It is also a time for celebrating the birth of the Christian church. Some churches celebrate Pentecost with a birthday cake and candles!

Jesus in different languages:

Chinese	耶稣
Dutch	Jezus
Finnish	Jeesus
French	Jésus
Italian	Gesù
Japanese	イエス
Spanish	Jesús
Swahili	Yesu

What Is Advent?

• • • • • • •

During the season of Advent, you can feel the excitement in the air. Christmas is coming! Carols play on the radio. Stores decorate with wreaths and colorful lights. For Christians, there is an even deeper excitement about what Christmas means.

Advent begins four Sundays before Christmas and ends on Christmas Eve. The word *advent* means "coming" or "arrival." Advent is a time when Christians remember that God sent His only Son, Jesus, to earth as a human baby (Luke 2:1–20). The arrival of Jesus was, and is, the most important event in human history. Advent is a time when Christians prepare their hearts for Christmas and remember God's great love for the world and all the people in it—including *you*!

To celebrate Advent, some Christians make a tabletop wreath of evergreens with five candles. The circle symbolizes eternity. The color green stands for God's everlasting life. Candlelight is a symbol of Jesus' victory over the darkness of evil, sin, and death and of His shining love (Romans 5:5).

Three purple candles symbolize hope, peace, and love. They are lit on the first, second, and fourth Sundays of Advent. The pink candle symbolizes joy. It's lit on the third Sunday of Advent. The fifth candle is white and stands tall in the middle of the Advent wreath. It symbolizes Jesus, and it is lit on Christmas Day. It's like a birthday candle for Jesus!

Is December 25 Really Jesus' Birthday?

• • • • • • •

No one knows for sure the exact day Jesus was born.

The decision to celebrate Jesus' birth in December came from Constantine the Great (AD 306–337), Rome's first Christian emperor. Life in ancient Rome was hard. People were superstitious and worshiped many false gods, including Sol, the sun god, and Saturn, the god of crops. The dark days of winter were a time of great worry. What if the sun never returned? Each year the Romans eagerly looked forward to the winter solstice on December 21, the shortest day of the year, after which the sun returned and the days grew longer.

For one week, beginning on December 17, they celebrated a festival called Saturnalia to welcome back the sun and longer days. They sang and danced and feasted. They decorated trees, a symbol of growth, with bits of shiny metal, and they gave gifts to each other. They celebrated the return of light to a cold, dark world.

Constantine loved Jesus. In many ways Jesus was like the sun. Jesus brought spiritual light into a dark world. Jesus warmed people's cold hearts. Constantine decided that no longer would Romans worship Saturn and the sun god. Instead, the Romans would worship God's Son! The first mention of celebrating Jesus' birthday on December 25 is in AD 336. The word *Christmas* comes from an early English phrase meaning "Mass of Christ." In the Roman church, *mass* means "worship service."

Today most Christians celebrate Christmas on December 25.* It's a happy, joyful time to celebrate God's love for all His children—including *you*!

*Because Eastern Orthodox Christians use a different church calendar, they celebrate Christmas on January 7.

Why Do We Give Gifts at Christmas?

• • • • • • •

In the days leading up to Christmas, more books, toys, games, clothing, and candy are advertised and sold than at any other time of year. Giving gifts to family and friends at Christmas is a loving thing to do. Receiving gifts is fun too! But sometimes we can get so excited about Christmas presents that we almost forget the reason we are giving and receiving them.

Yes, it is true that we give gifts to our family, friends, and teachers to show our love and appreciation for them. But at Christmas there is a deeper, even more important reason for gift-giving.

The Bible says that God loves to give good gifts to His human children (Matthew 7:11). We give gifts at Christmas to remind us of God's greatest gift to the world—His Son, Jesus.

We give gifts at Christmas to celebrate God's great generosity and love (John 3:16; Romans 6:23; 2 Corinthians 9:15; Ephesians 2:8, 3:7).

Who Are the Magi?

• • • • • • •

Traditional Christmas cards, carols, and pageants suggest that the Magi were three wise kings. But the Bible tells a slightly different story!

It is true that the Magi (*may*-jye) were wise men who followed a star on a long journey from Persia to Bethlehem. The word *magi* is the plural form of *magus*, a Latin word meaning "sorcerer." But Bible scholars think they were actually educated priests who were not Jewish but still recognized that Jesus was God's promised *messiah*, or "anointed one."

After Jesus was born, some wise men from the east came to Jerusalem.
—MATTHEW 2:1

There were at least two Magi, but there may have been more—perhaps many more! The Bible doesn't mention their names, or any camels either. The Bible also doesn't say Jesus was a newborn baby lying in a manger when the Magi arrived. The gospel writer Matthew says that Jesus was a "child" at home with His mother, Mary (Matthew 2:11). Maybe Jesus was walking and talking! Maybe when the Magi gave Him their gifts of gold, frankincense, and myrrh, He clapped His little hands and laughed with delight!

Why Did the Magi Give Jesus Gold, Frankincense, and Myrrh?

• • • • • • •

In the ancient world, these three costly items were used as gifts to honor powerful kings and *deities*, or pagan gods. Imagine how grateful and yet confused Mary and Joseph must have been by the Magi's arrival at their home with such special gifts.

So why gold, frankincense, and myrrh? They have deeply prophetic and symbolic meanings:

- **Gold** is a gift for kings, and Jesus is the King of kings (John 18:36; Revelation 1:5).
- **Frankincense** means "high-quality incense." Incense in Jesus' day was burned in the Jewish temple by priests as a symbol of their prayers going up to God (Psalm 141:2). Jesus is our one true Priest (Psalm 110:4).
- **Myrrh** means "bitter." It was burned as incense too, but was also used in the oil priests used to anoint God's holy prophets. In addition, myrrh was used in preparing bodies for burial. This bitter gift foreshadowed Jesus' suffering and death on the cross (Mark 15:23; John 19:39–40).

Many years passed before Mary and Joseph understood the deep meaning of these special gifts for Jesus. How amazed they must have been!

What Is Epiphany?

• • • • • • •

Epiphany (Ee-*pi*-fun-ee) is when Christians around the world celebrate the visit of the *Magi*, or wise men, who brought gifts to the young child Jesus (Matthew 2:1–11). Epiphany is also known as "King's Day" and the "Twelfth Day," because it takes place twelve days after Christmas. Epiphany reminds us that Jesus truly is God's Son.

The word *epiphany* means to "reveal" or "show." An epiphany is that "Aha!" moment when you suddenly understand something. It's like a light bulb coming on!

We remember the Magi at Epiphany because they were among the first people to understand that Jesus was sent to earth by God. Even though Jesus was just a small child, these very wise men recognized that He was divine. The word *divine* means "to come from God." Lots of stories in the Bible tells us about people having epiphanies and realizing that Jesus is God. You can have an epiphany too!

Was There Really a Star of Bethlehem?

Yes, there really was a star of Bethlehem. The Bible tells us that the Magi followed a star to Bethlehem in search of the Messiah.

Was the star of Bethlehem a sparkling meteor? A long-tailed comet? A brilliant supernova? In his book *The Christmas Sky*, astronomer Dr. Franklyn M. Branley suggests that the light in the heavens during Jesus' birth may have been one or more very unusual "wandering stars," or what we now know to be planets!

Like many biblical scholars, Dr. Branley believes that Jesus was probably born not in December, but in the springtime, sometime between 8 BC and 4 BC.

Today astronomers know how long it takes each planet to orbit the sun, so they can figure out the position of each planet in the sky at any time in human history. They can figure out precisely which "wandering stars" appeared above the horizon around the time of Jesus' birth! Isn't that amazing?

BEING A CHRISTIAN

When Does My Eternal Life Begin?

• • • • • • •

Oh, this is a very good question. And the answer may surprise you. Many people think that our eternal life doesn't begin until we die. But that's not so. You are living your eternal life right this very moment! How can this be?

God has no beginning and no end. This is because God, our Creator, is *eternal*—infinite or endless. God also planted eternity in your heart (Ecclesiastes 3:11). He knew and loved you *before* you were born (Psalm 139)! Because God, your Creator, is eternal, you are eternal too. Another word for your eternal identity is *soul*.

> **All the days planned for me were written in your book before I was one day old.**
>
> —PSALM 139:16

An old saying goes, "We're not human beings having a spiritual experience, but we are spiritual beings having a human experience." The truth is, we are *both*! We are fully human, and we are fully spiritual. The Bible says that when we die, our souls continue to live forever. And that's not all. Like Jesus, we will one day get brand-new bodies designed to live forever in heaven too.

Is It Okay to Fail?

• • • • • • •

No matter how hard we try, we all sometimes fail. It is part of being human. When we fail, we can experience crushing feelings of disappointment and discouragement. But God can use our failures to teach us important, unexpected lessons. Over time, He can even turn our failures into something beautiful and good!

Here are some of God's Bible promises to comfort and encourage you when you have tried very hard and failed:

- "The Lord upholds all who fall and lifts up all who are bowed down." (Psalm 145:14 NIV)
- "The godly may trip seven times, but they will get up again." (Proverbs 24:16 NLT)
- "We have troubles all around us, but we are not defeated. We do not know what to do, but we do not give up. We are persecuted, but God does not leave us. We are hurt sometimes, but we are not destroyed." (2 Corinthians 4:8–9)

Is It Okay to Be Angry?

• • • • • • •

Everyone feels angry sometimes. It is part of being human. The reason God wants you to "not let the sun go down while you are still angry" is so you can enjoy a good night's sleep and have good dreams (Ephesians 4:26 NIV). It is amazing how much better things can look in the morning!

Here are some of God's Bible promises to calm, comfort, and encourage you when you are angry:

- "It is better to be slow-tempered than famous." (Proverbs 16:32 TLB)
- "Always be willing to listen and slow to speak. Do not become angry easily. Anger will not help you live a good life as God wants." (James 1:19–20)
- "Don't get angry. Don't be upset; it only leads to trouble." (Psalm 37:8)
- "A gentle answer will calm a person's anger. But an unkind answer will cause more anger." (Proverbs 15:1)

When you are feeling angry, talk to God in prayer. It can also be helpful to talk to and pray with your mom or dad, or another trusted grown-up. Anger is a strong emotion, but it will pass. The good news is God's love stays with you forever!

"In your anger do not sin": Do not let the sun go down while you are still angry.

—EPHESIANS 4:26 NIV

Why Do I Still Sin When I Don't Want To?

• • • • • • •

God is perfect. People are not. Everyone makes mistakes. It is part of being human. Even the apostle Paul, who wrote the book of Romans, struggled mightily with sin! This is because Paul was human, just like you and me. And when Paul sinned, he absolutely hated it!

When you give in to temptation and sin, you feel guilty. The word *guilty* means to feel responsible (and probably a little ashamed) for having thought, said, or done something you know is wrong. Guilt is a very unpleasant and painful feeling. But that's okay. Sometimes painful feelings are God's way of protecting you! Like physical pain warns you of danger to your body, emotional pain warns you of danger to your soul.

> **I do not understand the things I do. I do not do the good things I want to do. And I do the bad things I hate to do.**
>
> —ROMANS 7:15

So when you sin and feel a pang of guilt, what can you do? Talk to God. *Confess*, or admit, your sin. Tell God you are truly sorry and you want to do better. Ask God to help you. Because Jesus died for your sins, God promises that He will forgive you. No matter what. Because He loves you that much!

What Is a Quiet Time?

God your heavenly Father is not a legend, myth, or fairy tale. He is alive and real, and He loves you—and He wants you to know Him! One way to do this is to set aside some time each day to spend with God—just the two of you. Some refer to this special, private meeting with God as a "quiet time."

When I was a little girl, I loved to sit on my father's lap, wrapped in his big, strong arms. We were very close, and I loved him so, so much. When he died, I thought my broken heart would never heal. One day, while praying to God, I cried, "Oh, Daddy, I miss my father so much!" *Daddy?* I thought. *Why would I ever call God "Daddy"?* But later I learned this was how Jesus prayed to God too! *Abba* in Jesus' native Aramaic language means "Daddy" or "Papa" (Mark 14:36).

Now when I have quiet time with God, I picture myself snuggled all cozy and warm on my heavenly *Abba* Father's lap, wrapped in His big, strong arms. You can love your quiet times with God too!

How Can I Make the Most of My Quiet Times?

• • • • • • •

There are no set rules for quiet times with God. The more time you spend with God, the better you'll get to know Him! Maybe start by setting aside ten to fifteen minutes each day to meet with God. The time of day doesn't matter. God is *always* available—every minute of every day! Here are a few tips for making the most of your special time with God:

- Be silent. Try to quiet your thoughts. Listen carefully for God.
- Pray. The more time you spend listening and talking to God, the better you'll get to know Him.
- Read your Bible. You'll be amazed how God can speak to you through the pages of His book!
- Write God a letter. Some people also use a prayer journal to keep track of prayer requests and answers.
- Read a daily devotional.

What Does It Mean to Count My Blessings?

• • • • • • •

When I was little, I remember my mom saying, "Whenever I'm feeling blue, I count my blessings." What is a blessing? It's anything that fills your heart with delight and gratitude.

Of course, no one is happy all the time. Because we're human, we all sometimes feel blue, and happiness and joy seem very far away. That's the time to count your blessings! It will fill your heart with thankfulness! One good way to count your blessings is to make a list. Here are ten blessings to get you started. Once you make your own list, you might discover that you have many more. *Happy counting!*

- I'm alive!
- God is real!
- God loves me!
- God has a special, unique purpose for my life!
- Jesus is real!
- God's Holy Spirit is real!
- Angels are real!
- Heaven is real!
- The Bible is true!
- God hears and answers my prayers!

Can I Have Friends Who Aren't Christians?

• • • • • • •

Yes, it is possible to be friends with people who don't know Jesus. God loves all His children. God wants us to love everyone too!

At the same time, remember that we are easily influenced by others. Good friends can be a good influence, and bad friends can be a bad influence. Jesus had lots of different kinds of friends. Some believed in Him. Some didn't. Some just didn't know what to think! Jesus didn't change when He was with different kinds of people. When people spoke or behaved badly, He didn't join in. He was always true to Himself and His Father God. He was honest and good. He was generous and kind. He was patient and forgiving. Most of all, He was loving.

The Bible teaches that we are ambassadors for Jesus here on earth. An *ambassador* is an official representative. As Christ's ambassador, the words you say and the way you act make a big impression on others—especially on friends who don't yet know Jesus.

Being an ambassador for Jesus comes with responsibilities.

How Can I Discover My God-Given Gifts and Talents?

• • • • • • •

How can you know what your God-given gifts and talents are? God has given you a way to discover His special gifts. He has already planted it in your heart. It's God's gift of enthusiasm (en-*thoo*-zee-az-um). *Enthusiasm* means "to be inspired and indwelled by God." That's why when you feel enthusiasm, it is a good idea to pay attention!

Ask yourself: What is it you love to do? What is it that excites and energizes you? Perhaps it is spending time with your grandma and grandpa . . . or playing on a sports team . . . or learning everything you can about a subject like astronomy, or dinosaurs, or computers . . . or reading . . . or spending time with little ones . . . or singing . . . or caring for animals . . . or painting . . . or making your friends laugh . . . or dancing . . .

Whatever it is, just follow your natural enthusiasm. There is only one you, and God has special plans for you. He loves to reveal to you His unique gifts and purposes for your life!

What Can I Do to Help People in Need?

• • • • • • • •

Our life on earth is a gift from God. God wants us to care about people in need. Jesus said, "Everyone who has been given much will be responsible for much. Much more will be expected from the one who has been given more" (Luke 12:48). Once we care about others, God asks us to do something more. He asks us to use our lives to reach out and help. This is called putting our Christian faith into action.

Here are a few ideas for how you can help people in need:

- You can pray for someone.
- You can visit an older person who is lonely.
- You can listen to your friend who is in trouble or sad.
- You can write an encouraging letter to a soldier far away from home.

She welcomes the poor.
She helps the needy.
—PROVERBS 31:20

Talk to your mom and dad, or your pastor or youth minister at church. They will have lots of good ideas too!

Why Is Taking Care of Our Planet Important?

God created our planet Earth and everything in it. God loves the world (John 3:16). God loves His children (1 John 3:1). God made everything in the world for His children.

He gives us water to drink. He gives us delicious fruits and vegetables, chicken and fish, and other foods to eat. He gives us trees and stone to build houses. He gives us coal, oil, gas, water, sunshine, and wind for power. What a generous Father God we have! God instructed humans to take care of His creation (Genesis 1:26, 2:15). Taking care of the earth is called *stewardship*, which means "to care for another's property."

Our beautiful planet doesn't belong to us. We didn't make it. It belongs to our Father God. Our job is to take good care of it. Christians believe it's important to keep our air and water clean and be careful with our natural resources like trees and oil. It's important not to litter. Why take good care of our planet? It's one way of saying "Thank You!" to God for His beautiful creation.

How Can I Share God's Love?

God has planned so many wonderful ways for you to share His love with others! It helps to remember that the good things God has planned for you to do always have to do with *love*. Need some ideas? You can be sure you are discovering God's special purposes for your life when you do things like these:

- Tell your parents you love them.
- Surprise your parents by unloading the dishwasher or setting the table.
- Hug your grandma and grandpa.
- Write your aunt a letter and tell her how much you love and miss her.
- Thank your teacher for working so hard.
- Invite the new kid in school to sit with you at lunch.
- Tell your friend you're sorry you hurt their feelings.
- Listen to your friend who is sad.
- Pray for your friend who is sick.
- Invite your friend to church or youth group.

Show God how much you love Him by trying to love and help others. I bet you can come up with lots more good ideas of your own. Have fun!

How Do I Tell a Friend About Jesus?

Good news is fun to share. And knowing Jesus is good news! If you have a friend who you think might want to know more about Jesus, don't be shy. Speak right up. When the disciples worried about what to say, Jesus promised that God's Holy Spirit would give them just the right words (Mark 13:11). So relax. When it comes to telling a friend about Jesus, all you have to do is speak honestly, from your heart.

You might want to share . . .

- How Jesus helps you in your day-to-day life
- How your prayers have been answered
- What you love about Jesus

Remember that Christianity is not just another religion. Christianity is a *relationship* with the living Jesus. It's also helpful to remember that Jesus is not a legend, myth, or fairy tale. The beginning of Jesus' story is in Luke 2:1–7, and it does not begin with "Once upon a time . . ." Jesus is *real*.

If your friend wants to ask Jesus into his or her heart, here is a simple prayer he or she can pray:

> *Jesus, I really want to know You. I believe You are the Son of God. I believe that You died for my sins. Thank You for loving me so much. Now please come into my heart and live in me. Amen.*

When your friend has prayed this prayer, encourage your friend to share this good news with his or her parents, pastor, youth minister, or other grown-up who loves Jesus. They will want to help your friend get to know Jesus better too.

What an honor it is to introduce a friend to Jesus!

BIG QUESTIONS

How Is It Possible for God to Truly Love Billions of Different People?

• • • • • • •

My friend Dr. Bill Wilson was a world-famous psychiatrist who also loved Jesus. One day I asked him this question.

"Good question!" He laughed. And then he grew thoughtful. "When I was training to be a doctor," he said, "I delivered many babies. One thing amazed me: no matter how long a mother is in labor, no matter how painful, the first thing she wants after giving birth is to see and hold her baby. This is because a new mother loves her child instinctively. It doesn't matter if it is her first, second, fifth, or twelfth child." Dr. Wilson smiled. "It's hard to imagine a love so strong. But here's the truth: God's love for us is even stronger! We are His children, and He knows and loves each one of us unconditionally—like a new mother."

How is it possible for God to truly love His billions of children in the world? Because God invented love. In fact, God *is* love (1 John 4:8). As our perfect heavenly Father, He loves each of us with an eternal love that never ever runs out. Never. Ever. This is very good news!

If God Loves People, Why Do Bad Things Happen?

• • • • • • •

Bad things happen because the world is not the way God originally created it. In the garden of Eden, there was no human pain, suffering, or death. But Adam and Eve chose to sin, and now the world and all the people in it struggle with being disordered and broken. For now, pain, suffering, and death are part of being human.

But God is good. The Bible says, "God is love" (1 John 4:8). He loves the world and all the people in it. We know God loves us because He sent His only Son, Jesus, to earth to die for our sins (Romans 5:8). God did this to make a way for us to never die, so we can live with Him forever in heaven (John 3:16). That's a whole lot of love!

We also know that God is not like us. God is perfect. We are not. God sees all of human history from heaven. We can only see here and now. "'For my thoughts are not your thoughts, neither are your ways my ways,' declares the LORD. 'As the heavens are higher than the earth, so are my ways higher than your ways and my thoughts than your thoughts'" (Isaiah 55:8–9 NIV). For now, there are many things about God we cannot understand. But because God is good, we can trust Him. Because God is good, we can accept His mysteries. And in heaven we will see everything clearly (1 Corinthians 13:12). But until then, bad things will happen. Remember: even though bad things still happen, God promises to help you through them. You are not alone. He hears and answers your prayers. He watches over you. He loves you. He promises that one day you will live with Him and Jesus and all the angels forever in heaven! And God always keeps His promises.

Is It Okay to Have Doubts About God?

Yes, it's okay to question and sometimes have doubts about God. Everyone does. Questioning God is not unbelief. It's the sign of a healthy, curious, human mind! God loves it when you're honest and bring Him all your questions and doubts. That's because God knows you inside and out and cares deeply about every detail of your life!

When you ask questions and admit your doubts, you're in good company. Many famous believers sometimes felt unsure about God. The apostle Thomas doubted Jesus had risen from the dead—until Jesus visited him in His resurrected body (John 20:24–29)! Saint John of the Cross, a sixteenth-century Spanish believer, called his time of doubt the "dark night of the soul." My favorite example comes from Jesus Himself. When Jesus was suffering on the cross, He cried out from the bottom of His heart: "My God, why have you left me alone?" (Mark 15:34). He was in terrible pain and felt totally cut off from His Father. But even then, Jesus never lost His faith. He never stopped asking God questions.

When you have doubts and questions about God, let Him know. God loves you dearly and is always eager to hear from you. His deepest desire is for you to know and love Him too.

Why Do People Hurt Other People?

• • • • • • •

Human beings are not perfect. People hurt other people for many reasons. Sometimes they're afraid, or sick, or sad. Sometimes people hurt others because they've been hurt themselves.

When I was little, I had a beautiful boxer named Roxie. Roxie belonged to another family before us. They used to go away on long trips and lock poor Roxie in their cold, dark basement while they were gone. Roxie didn't like that. She panicked and barked and scratched at the basement door. Sometimes she scratched the door so hard that her paws bled.

> "Love your enemies. Pray for those who hurt you."
> —MATTHEW 5:44

A few months after Roxie came to live with us, we had to go away on a trip. The minute Roxie saw my suitcase, she looked at me with panicky eyes and ran away! It took my dad an hour to catch her. I loved Roxie, and it hurt my feelings that she ran away. Did it mean she didn't love me? My dad explained that Roxie ran away because she was afraid. She had been hurt by her other owner, and she just didn't want to be hurt again.

There is a lot of wisdom in this old saying: "Be kind. For everyone you meet is carrying a heavy burden." People hurt one another, it is true. People are not perfect. But we can always pray and try to show each other love and kindness (John 13:34–35).

Can Anything Good Come Out of Pain and Suffering?

Everyone experiences pain and suffering in life. It's part of being human. God doesn't cause pain and suffering. But God can turn it into something beautiful, valuable, and good.

Think of a pearl, for instance. A pearl starts as a bit of sand that gets trapped in an oyster. The sand scratches and irritates the oyster, so it reacts by covering the sand with layers of protective coating. Over time, the sand becomes a beautiful pearl!

Sometimes we can have a difficult person in our life. When we cover the person with layers of love and prayers, they don't irritate us as much. The person may even become a beautiful friend! The best example of God turning pain and suffering into something beautiful and good is when God resurrected Jesus from His death on the cross. Because Jesus rose from the dead and received a resurrection body that can live forever in heaven, one day we will too!

Remember: God can turn *anything* into something beautiful and good!

Is Knowing Jesus the Only Way to Know God?

• • • • • • •

God is everywhere. Even when people have never heard about Jesus, they can know God as their Creator through the beauty of nature and the miracle of life. That's why thousands of years ago, the psalmist David wrote: "The heavens tell the glory of God. And the skies announce what his hands have made" (Psalm 19:1). Isn't that beautiful?

But there's an even deeper way of knowing God: through Jesus.

Jesus said, "If you really knew me, then you would know my Father, too" (John 14:7).

Yes, it's true that the only way to know God as our personal loving Daddy, or *Abba* Father, is through knowing His Son, Jesus.

> **"I am the way. And I am the truth and the life. The only way to the Father is through me."**
> **—JOHN 14:6**

Knowing Jesus is God's way for us to understand who He really is. Knowing Jesus is God's way for us to experience firsthand the reality and power of His forgiveness and love (John 3:16, 14:7).

Why Do People Have to Die?

• • • • • • •

For human beings, death is part of the natural order of things. This is because all earthly living things, including our human bodies, are mortal. The word *mortal* means "subject to death."

This is not what God originally intended. The Bible teaches that because of the choices made by the first man and woman, Adam and Eve, sin and death came into the world (Romans 5:12). For every person there is "a time to be born and a time to die" (Ecclesiastes 3:2). Still, no one wants to die. Death is sad for the people left behind. Because it's mysterious, the thought of death can be scary.

There is a right time for everything. Everything on earth has its special season. There is a time to be born and a time to die.

—ECCLESIASTES 3:1–2

Thanks to Jesus, you don't have to be sad or scared about death. Because you believe Jesus died for your sins and was raised from the dead, God promises that your sins are forgiven and you will live forever in heaven (John 3:16).

Why would God promise such a wonderful thing? Because God loves you. It's as simple as that.

Is It Okay to Feel Sad When Someone You Love Dies?

• • • • • • •

There is nothing that hurts more than when someone we love has died. This combination of sorrow and loss is called *grief*. Sadly, everyone eventually experiences grief. Grief is perhaps the most painful of all human emotions.

Here is good news: God understands. He feels your pain and wants to comfort you. It is okay to feel sad when someone dies and goes to heaven. It helps to remember that God is with you, even in your saddest and hardest moments.

Here are three of God's Bible promises for when you experience grief:

- "God will wipe away every tear from their eyes." (Revelation 7:17)
- "The Lord comforts his people." (Isaiah 49:13)
- "There will be no more death, sadness, crying, or pain. All the old ways are gone." (Revelation 21:4)

When you are feeling the pain and sorrow of grief, it can also be helpful to talk to and pray with others. They will understand and help you.

What Will Happen to Me When I Die?

• • • • • • •

Death, in some ways, is a lot like birth. Picture an unborn baby, all snug and warm in his mother's womb. For that baby, the thought of being born might be pretty scary.

If the baby could talk, he might say, "What? Are you kidding? You want me to leave my safe, warm world for someplace I know nothing about? *No way!*" He might be sad or scared. Maybe he's even angry. He might have the mistaken idea that what was about to happen to him wasn't birth, but death. After all, everything he ever knew about life so far was about to end.

Think how hard it would be to explain to him how wonderful life is on earth! How could you ever describe the brilliant colors of a rainbow? The smell of fresh-baked cinnamon bread? The taste of a chocolate ice cream cone with sprinkles? The fuzzy warmth of a puppy? The sound of laughter? The excitement of Christmas Eve? The way it feels to wake up on your birthday morning?

When your body dies, the Bible says that your soul joins Jesus and God and the angels in a wonderful new world called heaven. Heaven is a world that we, like an unborn baby, can hardly begin to imagine (1 Corinthians 2:9). But we can try!

What do you think heaven will be like?

Do People Who Have Never Heard of Jesus Go to Heaven Too?

• • • • • • • •

Not everyone has heard the good news about God's Son, Jesus. Many people lived and died before Jesus was born. Even today, with TV and the internet, millions of people still haven't heard about Jesus. We know from the Bible that God is perfect in every way—He's loving, wise, fair, and good. God knows the heart of every human. We can trust Him to make the right choice about who does or doesn't go to heaven, including those who have never heard of Jesus. God does not want you to worry about who gets to go to heaven. But you can do something about it!

- Love God and love others.
- Do your best to live a life that pleases God.
- Read God's Holy Word, the Bible.
- Share with others the good news about Jesus.
- Pray for the world and all the people in it.

Then, when you meet your Father God in heaven, He'll wrap His big, strong arms around you and say, "Well done!" (Matthew 25:23).

Will I See My Pet in Heaven?

• • • • • • •

Oh, what a good question! With human beings, the Bible is very clear about our future home in heaven (John 3:16). But when it comes to animals, the Bible is a little less clear. We do know that humans and animals are deeply connected, because we share the same loving Creator God.

Our pets are very special creatures, and we are all members of God's family of creation. Like Noah and the animals in the ark, we're all in the same boat!

To love an animal is a good and beautiful thing. What happens to the love we feel for our pets? The Bible says love never ends (1 Corinthians 13:8). It also promises, "No mere man has ever seen, heard, or even imagined what wonderful things God has ready for those who love the Lord" (1 Corinthians 2:9 TLB). Evangelist Billy Graham said, "God will prepare everything for our perfect happiness in heaven, and if it takes my dog being there, I believe he'll be there."

Will you see your pet in heaven? What do you think?

Are There Really Angels?

• • • • • • •

Yes, there really are angels. Thousands upon thousands of them (Hebrews 12:22)! The word *angel* means "messenger." The Bible says that God created the angels to be His personal messengers on earth (Hebrews 1:14).

Angels obey, worship, and praise God (Psalms 103:20, 148:2; Hebrews 1:6). Angels do not die (Luke 20:36). Angels are often described as beings of light. Because they can be so bright, angels are often pictured with golden halos around their heads (Matthew 28:3). Because they can appear and disappear so quickly, angels are often pictured with wings (Judges 6:21; Luke 1:11–12). Angels are very strong and powerful (2 Thessalonians 1:6–7; 2 Peter 2:11). They are neither male nor female. They do not marry or have baby angels (Matthew 22:30).

The Bible tells us that when angels appear to people, the first thing they often say is "Don't be afraid!" (Judges 6:23; Luke 1:13, 1:30). From this, we can assume that to see one of God's angels is awesome and frightening. But God's angels refuse to be worshiped by human beings (Revelation 19:10, 22:8–9). Sometimes, if it suits God's purposes, angels can appear as human beings (Hebrews 13:2)! Maybe this is so we won't be frightened.

In the Bible two of the angels, Gabriel and Michael, are given names. God sent Gabriel to deliver important messages (Daniel 8:15, 9:21; Luke 1:19, 1:26). The name *Gabriel* means "God is my strength." The name *Michael* means "Who is like God?" Michael is God's archangel, or "top-level" angel, who is a warrior for God

(Revelation 12:7). The Bible suggests there may be other archangels too (Daniel 10:13). In the future, when Jesus returns, He will come with many angels (Matthew 16:27).

The Bible says that God's angels are watching over us (Hebrews 1:14).

Are There Really Demons?

• • • • • • •

Yes, there really are demons.

Human beings live in a physical world. We experience the world through our physical senses. We see, touch, hear, smell, and taste our world.

But human beings also are surrounded by an invisible, spiritual world, where God the Father, Jesus, God's Holy Spirit, and all God's holy angels live. It is also a world where demons dwell (Mark 1:34, 1:39, 6:13).

Many biblical scholars believe that demons are angels that have turned against God.

The word *demon* means "evil spirit."

Angels are good. Demons are evil. Angels love God and all God's children. Demons hate God and all God's children. The leader of all the demons is Satan, who is a wicked angel. Throughout human history, God and His holy angels have been at war with Satan and his demons (Ephesians 6:12).

The good news is that thanks to Jesus, you do not need to fear Satan or his miserable demons (Romans 8:38–39). Through His death on the cross, Jesus has overcome Satan and his demons forever. Jesus has won the battle of good over evil for all time (1 Corinthians 15:57)!

Is the Devil Real?

• • • • • • •

Yes, the devil is real. Today he is known as Satan.

No one knows for sure how Satan came to be. Many biblical scholars believe that he started out as one of God's archangels named Lucifer (Isaiah 14:12 KJV). The name *Lucifer* means "morning star." Lucifer was the most beautiful, brilliant, and strong of all God's creatures in heaven. But Lucifer did not want to obey God. Lucifer wanted to be worshiped like God. Lucifer wanted authority and power that did not belong to him. Lucifer's sinful jealousy toward God turned to anger and hatred.

In his anger, Lucifer rebelled and took as many as one-third of heaven's angels with him to serve as his demons. Sometimes the Bible refers to angels as "stars." When Lucifer fell, his "tail swept a third of the stars [or angels] out of the sky and threw them down to the earth" (Revelation 12:4).

It is Satan who tempted Adam and Eve to sin in the garden of Eden. It is Satan who is still busy causing trouble in the world today. In the Bible, Satan is also called a dragon, a serpent, and the devil (Revelation 12:9). The word *devil* means "liar." The word *Satan* means "enemy" or "accuser."

Know this: Satan is nothing more than a furious, wicked angel. At the same time, Satan and his demons still have the power to cause much human heartache and misery. Satan is not only evil; he is very smart and tricky.

Jesus called Satan "a liar . . . and the father of lies" (John 8:44).

The apostle Peter warned, "Control yourselves and be careful! The devil is your enemy. And he goes around like a roaring lion looking for someone to eat" (1 Peter 5:8). *Yikes!*

The war Satan started between good and evil continues to this day. It is being waged in heaven and on earth, and it will continue until Jesus comes again with God's holy angels.

Thanks to the Bible, we know how the ongoing battle between good and evil ends. Happily, it is a very good ending! God's goodness, truth, justice, and peace win.

In the end, the Bible tells us that Satan and his demons will not go unpunished. The apostle Paul wrote, "In the end they will be punished for the things they do" (2 Corinthians 11:15). Finally, there will be peace in heaven and on earth.

Here is a big idea: because we know how the story ends, in a very real sense the battle has already been won! Because of Jesus' death on the cross for our sins and His resurrection, Satan has already been defeated. Even though we struggle with troubles and sin, with Jesus living in our hearts, we are "more than conquerors" (Romans 8:37–39 NIV).

Is Hell Real?

• • • • • • •

Yes, hell is real. Like heaven, hell exists outside time and space. Like heaven, sometimes there are glimpses of hell on earth. When people commit terrible acts of cruelty and murder, we get a glimpse of hell on earth. The terrible destruction and loss of human life caused by hurricanes, tornadoes, and tsunamis also give us glimpses of hell.

The word *hell* means "the underworld." The Bible teaches that hell is the final dwelling place for Satan, his demons, and the souls of human beings who choose to reject God's love. The Bible describes hell as a "lake of burning sulfur" (Revelation 20:10). It is also described as a place of "eternal fire" (Matthew 25:41 NIV). These descriptions suggest that hell is an experience of unending physical pain and torment. But hell is even worse than that.

Hell is a place of eternal separation from God and His love. It is a place of unbearable emotional pain. Think how it feels when you have a really bad stomachache. It hurts a lot. But a doctor can give you medicine to make the physical pain go away. Now think how you feel when a friend talks behind your back, or when a pet or loved one dies. The pain is much worse. There is no medicine to make emotional pain go away.

When Jesus was on the cross, He suffered for all the sins of everyone in the world.

He experienced hell for us. He experienced terrible physical pain. But the emotional pain Jesus suffered was far worse.

Jesus loved God with all His heart, soul, and mind. As He was dying on the cross, the thought of being separated from God forever was almost more than Jesus could bear. He cried out, "My God, my God, why have you forsaken me?" (Matthew 27:46 NIV; Mark 15:34 NIV).

But in the end, God did not forsake Jesus. God raised Jesus from the dead! Jesus ascended to heaven to sit at the right hand of God.

Thanks to God's great love, when you die, you will not go to hell. Because God sent Jesus to die for your sins, and because you love Jesus, you will go to heaven and live forever with God and His holy angels.

Why would God do such a wonderful thing? Because God loves you (John 3:16, 15:13; Romans 5:8; 1 John 3:1). It's as simple as that.

What Is Heaven Like?

• • • • • • •

Heaven has been in existence since before the creation of earth and human beings. Heaven exists outside our time and space. Heaven is home for God the Father; His Son, Jesus; God's Holy Spirit; and God's holy angels. Heaven is also home for the souls of all human beings who know and love God. Heaven is *your* eternal home (2 Corinthians 5:1)!

Another word for heaven is *paradise*, which comes from a Greek word that means "garden." Some people think heaven is like the garden of Eden, before Adam and Eve were tempted by Satan to sin. The Bible also describes heaven as a spectacular eternal city known as the "new Jerusalem" (Revelation 21:2). The Bible says heaven is so bright that it "does not need the sun or the moon to shine on it. The glory of God is its light" (Revelation 21:23).

We know from the Bible that heaven is a wonderful place full of love, peace, forgiveness, and joy. In heaven there is no more death, sadness, crying, or pain. In heaven, God will wipe away every tear from every eye (Revelation 7:17, 21:4).

And that's just the beginning. In heaven, we will get brand-new bodies! Here on earth, our human bodies aren't designed to last forever. Over time, they get old and worn out, or they meet with a sudden illness or accident. But our souls never die. The Bible says that in heaven our souls will be wrapped in new bodies—very special bodies that will never get sick, never feel pain, and never get old. They are bodies that will live forever (1 Corinthians 15:42, 15:52–54; 2 Corinthians 5:1; 1 Peter 1:23)!

How all this happens is very wonderful and mysterious. "Listen," the apostle Paul wrote, "I tell you this secret: We will not all die, but we will all be changed. It will only take a second. We will be changed as quickly as an eye blinks" (1 Corinthians 15:51–52).

Sometimes God gives us glimpses of heaven on earth.

Heaven is the way it feels in our hearts when we love someone. Heaven is the way it feels in our hearts when we know deep down inside that we are loved back.

How wonderful heaven will be (1 Corinthians 2:9)!

About the author

KATHRYN "KITTY" SLATTERY is a longtime contributing editor for *Guideposts magazine* and the author of several books for children and adults, including *If I Could Ask God Anything*, *365 Bible Answers for Curious Kids*, *My Friend Jesus*, *Heart Songs*, *Lost & Found*, *The Gospel for Kids*, *Grandma I'll Miss You*, *The Grace to Grow*, and *A Bright Shining Place*. Her writing has appeared in ParentLife, Today's *Christian Woman*, *Angels on Earth*, *All Creatures*, and many other publications. Kitty and her husband live in Bedford, New Hampshire, and Vero Beach, Florida. They are the parents of two grown children and one beloved grandchild. Visit Kitty and learn more about her work at www.KathrynSlattery.com.